THE

# Destruction of Nature

IN THE

# Soviet Union

Boris Komarov

# THE
# Destruction
# of Nature
# IN THE
# Soviet Union

FOREWORD BY MARSHALL I. GOLDMAN

M. E. Sharpe, INC.
WHITE PLAINS, NEW YORK

Russian text world copyright © by Possev-Verlag, V. Goracheck K. G., 1978, Frankfurt/Main. Boris Komarov, *Unichtozhenie prirody, Obostrenie ekologicheskogo krizisa v SSSR.*

English text © 1980 by M. E. Sharpe, Inc., 901 North Broadway, White Plains, New York 10603

Translated by Michel Vale and Joe Hollander.

**Library of Congress Cataloging in Publication Data**

Komarov, Boris.
    The destruction of nature in the Soviet Union.

    Translation of Unichtozhenie prirody.
    Includes bibliographical references and index.
    1. Pollution—Russia. 2. Ecology—Russia.
I. Title.
TD186.5.R9K6513     363.7'32'0947     80-5452
ISBN 0-87332-157-X

Printed in the United States of America

# Contents

# Foreword

BY MARSHALL I. GOLDMAN

While several authors have periodically criticized one specific aspect of Soviet environmental life or another, no Soviet author has officially published an overall analysis of the problem. Until now the overall analysis has been written primarily by Western scholars who, as diligent as they might be, inevitably have had no access to information about some of the more serious environmental abuses that have occurred. For that reason the appearance in the Soviet Union of *The Destruction of Nature* by Boris Komarov is an important event.

His book, even though it appeared through unofficial samizdat channels, does seem to be an authentic study. There is no one outside the Soviet Union who could have had access to the information he has. Some of the incidents he cites are known only to Soviet citizens and have never been officially acknowledged by Soviet authorities. Unfortunately, even Soviet officials seem to have incomplete information about what is happening to the Soviet environment, and therefore it is entirely possible that even Komarov omits much that is important. Indeed, that seems to be the overall theme of his study: that in the absence of public knowledge of ecological problems, it is very difficult to muster public or official support for the correction of environmental abuses. He estimates that over 85 percent of the Soviet population is ignorant of how serious the conditions are. Thus it is particularly interesting to learn of the official Soviet ban placed on the publication and discussion of environmental problems in 1971 and 1972.

Although the general public is mostly unaware of what has happened, the scientific community has kept more or less abreast. Several commissions have been established to investigate the effects of various projects and also to make general surveys of the environmental situation. Komarov mentions some of them, including the Sokolov Commission on Lake Baikal which urged more careful handling of the lake. Even more stunning were the two nationwide studies *Priroda 1980* and *Priroda 1990* [Nature 1980 and 1990], which projected environmental conditions into the future. Their forecasts were very gloomy; but even though they were made available to Gosplan, the Soviet planning agency, their appearance did not seem to set off any significant corrective measures. Moreover, such measures will probably not be forthcoming until the public is informed about such problems, and that is unlikely as long as such reports are kept secret.

There seem to be two reasons for the Soviet passion for secrecy——military or strategic considerations and simple embarrassment. It was for military reasons that Gosplan felt it necessary to push for an increase in the production of cellulose. This in turn led to the construction of two cellulose plants at Lake Baikal. That there were alternatives to this decision, such as the construction of the cellulose plants at other less sensitive sites or the use of petroleum as a base for making cellulose, was not adequately publicized because the military sector was the main force demanding the use of the cellulose. Similarly, all hazards associated with atomic energy have been censored because of the military importance of atomic energy and weapons. It is usually sufficient for a scientist to say that there is nothing to fear——when the state insists, it is reassurance enough. What is not admitted, however, is that there have been some very serious incidents, including one in 1958 near Cheliabinsk in which mishandling of atomic wastes made an area within a radius of 200 kilometers radioactive.

Strategic considerations also led to the official denial that PCBs were even being produced in the Soviet Union. To acknowledge such a fact would have revealed that the Soviets were producing equipment with military potential. For the same reason the Soviet Union has refused to support a worldwide project designed to provide an inventory of waste discharges. Proposed by Professor Wassily Leontief, formerly of Harvard and now at New York University, such a study would have made it possible to prevent undue buildups of potentially hazardous materials. The United States, along with most of the rest of the world, supported the idea, but the Soviets feared that the release of such data would make it possible for foreigners to determine Soviet production activities as well as inefficiencies. Undoubtedly this is so, but it would also make possible a worldwide environmental effort. Without input from the Soviet Union, such a project has been severely handicapped.

Another important reason for Soviet secrecy is that Soviet officials are simply embarrassed by some of their environmental incidents. Of course, such motivation is not unique to the Soviet Union. Oil spills everywhere are an embarrassment, as are air pollution incidents, including those that lead to death and an increase in the cancer rate. Komarov amply documents such incidents in the Soviet Union.

Komarov highlights some of the other difficulties in dealing with Soviet environmental problems, some of which are unique to the Soviet Union. In contrast to the United States, for instance, attempts to correct environmental disruptions will be frustrated as long as responsibility for the administration of the environmental control industry and control of pollution itself are not separated. At the present time Gosplan is ultimately responsible for both activities as well as increasing industrial production. The Hydrometeorological Committee, which attempts to administer some pollution control efforts, simply lacks the clout necessary to shut down industries. Therefore Gosplan is its own judge of when pollution problems are serious, and usually it comes down on the side of more production.

In the same way the union republics of the USSR find themselves with little authority over the larger industrial all-union ministries in Moscow. The union ministries frequently take the lead in trying to adopt more effective controls, but all too often they find that the affiliates of the Moscow ministries pay no heed to local complaints. They seek refuge instead in the central power that emanates from Moscow.

Komarov also identifies himself strongly with those who resent the growing Soviet involvement with the outer world, especially when it necessitates the export of valuable raw materials. He opposes the sale not only of Soviet oil and gas but of Soviet timber and cotton. In particular he is concerned that to procure timber, the delicate ecological balance of the Far North must be upset, while to grow cotton, immense irrigation projects are required that necessitate the disruption of existing ecological patterns all over the country.

But as revealing and outspoken as Komarov is, there are nonetheless some shortcomings in his book. In the first place, he makes some mistakes. In his excellent chapter on the problems of Lake Baikal, he reports that the first mention of significance about the impending construction of the cellulose plants at Lake Baikal appeared in an April 1963 article in the journal *Oktiabr'* [October]. That is incorrect. A pamphlet about the problem was issued as early as 1960 and a book in 1961. However, both were printed in the Siberian city of Ulan-Ude, and it is unlikely that very many Soviet policy-makers had access to the material. However, a letter to the editor did appear in *Komsomolskaia pravda* [Communist Youth League Pravda] in December 1961, as did an article discussing the problem in *Ekonomicheskaia gazeta* [Economic Newspaper] in January 1962. This evidently shows that even specialists in the Soviet Union have trouble obtaining access to all the materials.

Finally, although there is much that Komarov can justifiably complain about, he does seem to be harsher than necessary. He is most reluctant to acknowledge any progress in coping with the problem. If he mentions any Soviet success, it is normally only to show how the Soviets cover up what is really happening. But this is unfair. While admittedly the Soviets have a long way to go, they have at least come to recognize the problem and are beginning to seek some remedy. Thus, as bad as water pollution may be in most Soviet cities, in many instances the situation is better now than it was a few years ago. For instance, fish have returned to the Moscow River, and the air is much better in many Soviet cities than it was in the 1950s—if for no other reason than the switch from coal to natural gas and oil as a source of electrical power and heat. This has made an enormous difference, and the failure to spend much time on such improvements leaves the impression that Komarov may be leaning over backward to compensate for the traditional emphasis on how successful the Soviets have been. Yet his other insights are fascinating, and the study will be an important addition to our information about the USSR.

Marshall I. Goldman

THE
# Destruction of Nature
IN THE
# Soviet Union

# 1 A Distant Cloud

In April 1963 the Soviet press carried the first disquieting essay about Baikal in the magazine *October*. The author of the essay, V. A. Chivilikhin, wrote that two huge paper and pulp combines, the construction of which had already begun on the shores of Lake Baikal, were threatening to quickly poison the unique lake and grind all the forests around it into cellulose.

"If the projected construction plans are carried out, what will this mean—goodbye Baikal?" asked Chivilikhin. He answered: "No one wants to believe it. The disease can still be cured, and Baikal, that radiant orb of Siberia, will be healthy again . . . the people of communism will again be able to draw from its full, pure cup all its bounty."

Chivilikhin's statement was followed by articles in *Pravda*, *Komsomol Pravda*, and other magazines and newspapers.

The story of Baikal had begun. By 1963 it had become clear that Progress had begun to seriously menace nature on that sixth part of the earth's surface colored red on the globe.

The press was strewn with proposals for saving Baikal. It turned out that even before 1963, the majority of experts had opposed the construction of the paper and pulp combines: the Conference on the Development of the Productive Forces of Siberia; the Congress of Siberian Geographers; the Botanical Institute of the Academy of Sciences of the USSR; the Zoological Institute of the Academy of Sciences; the Third Congress of the Geographical Society of the USSR; the Moscow Society of Naturalists; the All-Union Society of Hydrobiologists; and the All-Union Society of Microbiologists; and finally, the Siberian Division of the Academy of Sciences. This went on for more than four years, from 1958 through 1962.

The State Planning Committee (Gosplan) of the USSR and

the Committee on Forestry and the Paper and Pulp Industry paid not the slightest heed to all of these opinions and continued construction of the combines.

The situation resembled the famous scene with Grinev in *The Captain's Daughter.*

> "Do you see that?" The coachman pointed to the east with his whip.
> "I don't see anything except the white steppes and the clear sky."
> "No, way over there: that cloud."
> And in fact on the horizon I saw a small white cloud that at first I had taken for a distant knoll. The coachman told me that the cloud foretokened a storm.

As we know, Grinev continued on his way nevertheless.

"To allow these factories will be a gross, irrevocable historical mistake," wrote the chairman of the Vologodshchina collective farm, Ivan Sysosev.

"This is a sad, lamentable example of planning the development of one branch of industry at the expense of others" (Sharoev, a graduate student, Alma Ata).

"We must take into account the moral damage done by such projects in developing industry" (Prozorovskii, engineer, Moscow).

"The Soviet public is upset about the leveling of the thick taiga around Lake Baikal and the construction of the paper and pulp combines . . ." (Zenkevich, corresponding member of the Academy of Sciences, Moscow).

"Baikal is not only a priceless basin of living water but also a part of our souls," declared the professional rhetorician, Leonid Leonov.

"Baikal has been turned into an experimental reservoir for testing sewage treatment systems, systems not tested in production, to say nothing of the severe climatic conditions of the Trans-Baikal Region." Academicians Trofimuk, Kapitsa, Burg, Artsimovich, Gerasimov, Zeldovich, Petrianov, Emanuel, Kazanskii, Melentev, and Konstantinovskii, one of the vice-presidents of the Academy at the time, wrote in their sharply critical but deeply personal opinions.

Neither Siberian nor Moscow scientists were allowed access to the project documents for the Baikal combine, which was much larger (larger?) than the second, the Selenginskii, combine and was started first as planned. The inquiries of the Siberian Division of the Academy of Sciences of the USSR, and later of the Moscow Academy, to the Committee on Forestry went unanswered.

On what basis was construction begun? Who did the preliminary survey and estimates and how? The Soviet public never saw these materials, without which any serious discussion of the projects and their consequences was impossible.

After a special resolution of the Council of Ministers of the USSR, a few scientists were permitted to look at the documents from the expert evaluations made by the State Planning Committee of the RSFSR, which had approved the program for the construction of the Baikal combine. In these papers they found in particular such gems as: "The sewage water will create conditions for the propagation of life within the radius they cover, and this will mean an increase, rather than a decrease, in fish reserves"(!).[1] It is not surprising that these papers were so assiduously concealed from outside eyes.

Three years after the campaign began, Chivilikhin publicly proclaimed: "Like many others, I gnashed my teeth over Baikal; but to the great chagrin of thousands upon thousands, all the earlier decisions about Baikal remained in effect."

At the Twenty-third Congress of the Communist Party of the Soviet Union, also in 1966, Mikhail Sholokhov was still able to suggest: "Perhaps we will find the strength to renounce felling the forests around Baikal and the construction there of cellulose enterprises, and instead build some that will not endanger the purity of the lake. Later generations will not forgive us if we do not conserve this glorious sea, our blessed Lake Baikal."

But the Baikal combine was already set.

The wave of sincere, spontaneous indignation that Baikal generated never appeared in the official Soviet press either before or after. Initially the problem had nothing to do with politics, but gradually the mindless position of Gosplan and the Committee for the Forestry Industry, as well as the total disregard for "the voice of the people," ignited purely political passions. The word "Baikal" sounded an alarm in the international press as well.

Something had to be done. The fate of the lake became a case in which the authorities had to reassure people and not command them simply to be quiet, simply to shut up.

And people were not simply shut up. It was announced that the most sophisticated and most expensive treatment facilities in the world would be built at the Baikal combines. A special commission was set up by the Presidium of the Academy of Sciences in Moscow, which was not long in confirming authoritatively that the measures undertaken by the government to protect Baikal were effective and on the whole adequate. This was in late 1966.

A number of articles and films followed, creating the impression among the broad public that some Solomon's solution had been found, some balance, and that even if the combine did pollute the lake, it would not do so badly, not catastrophically.

In 1977, ten years after the combine had begun operation, a new special commission of the Academy of Sciences of the USSR on Baikal, with Academician V. E. Sokolov as chairman, presented a report which showed that the danger of Baikal being destroyed had increased rather than decreased, that the entire lake was on the brink of irreversible changes.

There is nothing surprising here. Ten years ago, to placate public opinion, not only were treatment plants constructed but even more effective measures were taken.

One after the other, resolutions were adopted restricting information about Baikal. The first, in late 1963, was evidently a personal decision by Khrushchev himself; the second was in the late '60s; and the third, in 1975, covered not only information about the condition of Baikal but any ecological information in the mass press throughout the country. Now one sees almost no facts or figures on industrial exploitation of the Baikal region. On the other hand, in "general review" articles Baikal has become "evidence of socialism's concern for the natural environment." The millions invested in the Baikal sewage treatment facilities have had a trivial biological effect, but the propaganda gains from them have been beyond expectations.

None of the hundreds of thousands of people living near Baikal nor the thousands of tourists who enjoy the lake know anything about the work of the Sokolov Commission nor about the deadly peril that is accumulating gradually and silently, like an avalanche, in the depths of Baikal.

There is little hope that the perilous situation of Baikal will become known to the public in the near future. Just as it still knows nothing about the work of the first Academy of Sciences Baikal Commission, which forecast and predicted all of the lake's present woes. That story explains much of the current situation.

The behind-the-scenes part of the Baikal story——or more accurately tragedy——went as follows.

The Academy of Sciences Commission addressed the "Baikal problem" only after tens of millions of rubles had already been invested in the Baikal paper and pulp combine (BPPC). Behind the Committee on the Forest Industry, the body officially in charge of the combine, stood the military. At that time the Ministry of Defense needed new durable cord for heavy bomber tires. Such things are referred to tersely as "strategic interests of the country" and are not subject to discussion even within the Council of Ministers. The immunity of the Baikal projects to any criticism is explained by these "strategic interests." They had sealed Baikal's fate by 1959.

For several years durable cord had been purchased from Sweden and Canada, but of course we had to have our own; and when the question of constructing a combine arose, there were two options: Lake Ladoga or Baikal. The point was that the production technology of this type of cord required huge quantities of very clean water.

The Leningrad Regional Committee categorically opposed construction on Lake Ladoga, since the lake was already surrounded by much industry; and moreover, Ladoga was in the foreseeable future still to be the chief source of drinking water for Leningrad and its suburbs from Pargolovo to Gatchina.

Baikal, on the other hand, is formally in the Buryat Autonomous SSR. Buryatia still had to make the leap into the twentieth century——from feudalism to socialism——and this circumstance sealed the fate of the lake once and for all.

The huge combine would mean only advantages for underdeveloped Buryatia, ranging from the flattering status it would acquire by hosting a strategic industry to better——one category higher——supply of the population with goods throughout the entire area around the combine.

Industrial development remains the slogan, the ideal, the sole absolute value in the eyes of any Soviet leader to this very day. Let alone the early sixties . . .

When G. I. Galazii, the director of the Baikal Limnological Institute, spoke in defense of the lake, First Secretary of the Buryat Regional Committee Modagoev publicly called him an "enemy of the people." This was 1963, but even after the Twenty-second Congress such accusations had an air of seriousness about them. To be sure, Modagoev had added "enemy of the Buryat people. . . ."

The plans for the Baikal combine provided for no treatment facilities whatsoever, and there is no doubt that the combine would have begun operations in this form under the pressure of the Regional Committee, with its vested interests, had it not been for an unexpected public outcry.

The indefatigable Galazii was also appointed to the specially created commission of the Academy of Sciences on Baikal, that Areopagus of sages which was supposed to present the people with its objective opinion on the problem. Eminent specialists from Irkutsk, Leningrad, and Moscow were members of the commission. Its chairman was Academician Gerasimov, director of the Institute of Geography.

All the conditions had been created for the commission's operation, but they did not last long . . .

A few years later one of the commission members observed:

> Every form of cooperation was accorded us. All the institutes and laboratories met our requests without delay. About a half year later we submitted our report to the vice-president of the Academy of Sciences, A. P. Vinogradov.
>
> He took a look at our conclusions and immediately sent the report back to us.
>
> "You maintain that the Baikal combines will prove fatal to the lake. But how can this be? The government decides to build, and you say 'impossible. . . .' Take your report and do some work on it."
>
> That is when the real arm twisting began. Elementary arithmetic showed that even after treatment effluents containing dissolved matter each year would dump more than 30,000 tons of sodium sulfides and chlorides, toxic lignin, foul-smelling mercaptan compounds, and the like into Baikal. The concentration of mineral compounds in the waste waters after purification would be thirty to forty times higher than the normal Baikal levels. How could this not have an effect on the sensitive Baikal flora and fauna when many of them cannot even live in the Angara, where the water is only slightly worse than in Baikal?
>
> There was, it seemed, no way out. Neither the Presidium of the Academy of Sciences nor Vinogradov could object to our work. But no means were spared. To oppose our commission the Presidium created its own commission, consisting of chemists. At its head they put Zhavoronkov, an academician, secretary of the Chemistry Department, a government man who knew what the Presidium needed.[2]
>
> Zhavoronkov himself had never been concerned with problems of sewage treatment. Some of his co-workers at the institute had studied this problem at Baikal and had come to the conclusion that it was unrealistic to neutralize foul-smelling, highly mineralized effluents.

Zhavoronkov had been present when they reported to the institute and had raised no objections. But later, at a meeting of the presidium, he began to claim that treatment of the BPPC effluents was so good that they were made harmless for the lake.

"But if Zhavoronkov himself says they are safe," declared Vinogradov to our commission, "how can you object! You're not chemists, not specialists."

Baikal specialists could be anyone you wished, just not us.

Physicists and mathematicians from the academy (mainly those who at that particular moment needed something from the presidium) were invited to the discussion of the reports of the commission. Support for Zhavoronkov or any reproof sent our way—these were services the functionaries of the presidium would not forget.

At one such meeting one old academician began to scream at us: "But why are we going on so about this Baikal? Pollute it if we have to. Now we have nuclear energy, and if later we have to, we can easily make a big pit and fill it with water, and that's it. We'll make Baikal again."

This nonsense resounded under the vaults of the Academy of Sciences, yet the vaults of our Temple of Science did not crumble. No one even chased out this senile academician. The meeting went on and the attacks on us continued. I repeat, this was a time of real arm twisting . . .

The second version of the commission's report was rejected, just like the first. The same happened to the third. Finally, in a fourth report the authors gave up their categorical conclusion that "construction would be ruinous for the lake." However, this concession was contingent on a number of measures: building a pipeline to dispose of waste waters over a ridge into the Irkut River, the creation of a national park and extensive restricted zones around the lake where no wood pulp would be processed, and so on.

As was to be expected, after fundamental agreement was reached on the operation of the BPPC, none of these conditions was met. Today, in 1977, almost all of them are in the discussion and design stage.

Several years after the Baikal incident in the Presidium of the Academy of Sciences, Academician Fedorenko was heard to boast among friends: "I did not destroy Baikal. I wasn't your Zhavoronkov. I never signed anything then. I got myself into the hospital. . . ."

The criminality of what they were doing to Baikal was clear to the academicians twelve years ago. Any appeals to ignorance, to the "tricks of technical progress" miss the point here.

As we noted, in 1975-76 the report of the second commission of the Academy of Sciences on Baikal was compiled and presented to the Council of Ministers of the USSR. The conclusions of this report with regard to the Baikal paper and pulp combine concurred with the opinion of the first commission: the combine had to be shut down and reequipped for environmentally safe production. Even the most expensive treatment equipment basically altered nothing; it merely transformed wholesale pollution into pollution of Baikal in installments.

The report begins with a central point—the tiny crustacean "epishura." Epishura lives only in Baikal and is the first link in the food chain of all the fauna of the lake. It constitutes 98 percent of all the mass of zooplankton on the north side of the lake and somewhat less on the south. In other words, epishura is the base of the pyramid at the top of which we find the unique Baikal varieties of whitefish, cod, grayling, and seal.

But epishura is not only an irreplacable food, it is also an extremely potent biological filter. Together with diatomic algae, it extracts about 250,000 tons of calcium per year from the waters of the rivers flowing into Baikal. Epishura is responsible for the unique purity of the Baikal water and, what is more, for its saturation with oxygen even in winter. Moreover, epishura cannot live anywhere but Baikal; it cannot survive even in pure Baikal water in a laboratory test tube.

Epishura died in the effluents from the paper and pulp combine (supposedly treated). It even died when the effluents were diluted 20, 60, and 100 times. The eggs and the larvae of the salmon also died in these tests.

Epishura is today becoming extinct in the waters several square kilometers around the BPPC. The young, whose numbers have been reduced by 80 percent, have especially suffered. Colonies of *Rotifera* worms, as sure a sign of water pollution as the nettle is on land, have sprung up on the bottom.

Spots of lignin, hydrogen sulfide products, and nonsulfate sulfur cover more than twenty square kilometers of the bottom, and their area is growing.

Algae have begun to flourish in the southern part of Baikal, something that had been considered impossible in its extremely pure waters. M. M. Kozhov, the renowned hydrobiologist, has shown that the biomass of algae in Proval Bay has increased fivefold in the last few years and is continuing to grow.

There were no effective enemies of the helminths in the lake. Their eggs now enter the lake waters from the effluents of the settlements and resorts along the shore, and the infestation of fish and animals has sharply increased. Sometimes nine of ten *omul* salmon caught by ichthyologists are teaming with worms.

Combine effluents would have caused much less harm if the treatment equipment had functioned smoothly, as it should have theoretically. But breakdowns constantly occur, and during these periods the sewage entering the lake is hundreds of times more toxic.

Pollution has even begun to interfere with the operations of the combine itself. It now extracts water that it has polluted itself and is unable to do the job it was built for——produce a specially durable cord for tires. However, this no longer bothers anyone——since 1964, before the BPPC had been completed, such cord has been made from petroleum.

The combine cannot even manage ordinary cord: instead of the 240,000 tons planned, it produces 160,000. In addition the BPPC furnishes the nation with 3,000 tons of packaging paper, 100,000 tons of nutrient yeast, and a little turpentine and tall oil.

Durable cord can now be made almost anywhere, in any part of the country. What then justifies the destruction of the priceless Baikal taiga? Why are we slowly but surely destroying the most precious body of water on the planet?

To produce a small proportion of the nation's cord, to maintain a few pig farms (they use the yeast), for a negligible amount of coarse packaging paper——the kind used to wrap nails ——and for an equally trivial amount of varnishes and paints (for which the tall oil and turpentine are used). And that is all.

And that we are indeed destroying the lake can no longer be doubted. We can equip plants to breed the whitefish and sturgeon; we can improve sewage treatment to some degree; but we cannot force epishura to live anywhere except in genuine, pure Baikal water. We can treat, so to speak, the blossoms and leaves of the Baikal tree as they should be treated or "á la Zhavoronkov"; but nothing can replace epishura——the root of the tree, its basis. How much must the numbers of this crustacean be reduced to upset the balance of the whole lake, for deterioration to become avalanchelike? No one can determine this exactly. But strictly speaking, such determinations amount to a discussion of what Baikal will become given our present methods of exploitation: an ordinary reservoir crawling with roaches, where greenish brown foul-smelling algae flourish, or something a little bit better?

The conclusions of the Baikal commission also point out other sources of pollution of the lake: the tons of bark that fall into the water when logs are floated by BPPC and then decompose to pollute it with lignin; the excessive felling of timber around the lake. The commission skirts the question of the true scale of this logging, the real harm it has inflicted on the "bright orb of Siberia." The truth of the matter is, however, that the conservation area extends only to the shore strip of taiga, only to what can be seen from the lake and admired by Soviet and foreign tourists. Just beyond the passes of the shore ridges begin continuous logging zones.

The light conifer taiga around Lake Baikal is almost as effective a biological filter as epishura. It cleanses sediments and effluents of many contaminants and microorganisms throughout the entire drainage area. After logging this filter no longer exists, while soil erosion from the mountain slopes promptly increases by 100 to 200 times. In the very first year as much as one fifth of the entire soil layer is carried away.[3] Once-crystalline rivulets and streams become turbid and dump millions of tons of organic and inorganic impurities into Baikal. Neither epishura nor diatomic algae can cope with this additional load.

Hundreds of square kilometers of beautiful taiga have already been cleared to meet the needs of the combine. Fellings and fires on the eastern slope of the Trans-Baikal ranges have clogged up many streams and even major rivers, such as the Olentui, and turned them into veritable sewers.[4]

A huge number of fires in the Baikal taiga can also be traced to negligence and inefficient methods of exploitation. In the summer of 1975 the builders of a highway in the Barguzin District set an old larch on fire to drive a squirrel out of a hollow in the tree. Several thousand hectares were burned as a result. In a government resolution on the rational utilization of natural resources in the Baikal Basin (1966), the slogan "cut one tree—plant two" was cited as the guideline for the development of this region. During the same period Chivilikhin wrote that in one dry summer more forest was burned down in Irkutsk Province alone than was planted in one year in all ninety provinces of the Russian Federation. We have no current statistics, but in the opinion of experts, the figure of one hectare of trees planted for each one hundred hectares destroyed is most realistic.

Experts have testified that in the period just passed (summer 1977, spring 1978), some major new fires occurred in the northern Baikal area. Hundreds of thousands of hectares of taiga (it appeared from the air) were burned out around the very beautiful mountain Lake Frolikh and the river of the same name. The Lower Angara Forestry Enterprise is routinely felling timber along Cape Kotelnikov, Cape Pongane, and around the Severo-Baikalsk and Kholodnyi settlements—in places long proposed as reserves. The forestry industry will try to snatch what it can while the defenders of nature struggle to overcome countless administrative barriers.

The forest burns because of the campfires of geologists, builders, hunters, and tourists. The taiga around Lake Baikal has been comparatively well restored since logging, but the flamability of saplings in the taiga deciduous forests is comparable only to that of gunpowder. Hundreds of experts have worked on the problem of the flamability of the Trans-Baikal taiga. But none of them has been able to suggest anything better than what the famous biologist, the elder Skalon, proposed at the beginning of the century. The chief source of forest fires is man, he said; hence the only way to preserve the Baikal taiga is to strictly bar it to random irresponsible people. It is neither easy nor cheap to let in only a limited number of trained experts whose presence in the taiga is quite necessary. However, this is the only way that can produce results.

"But is there any taiga left worth saving?" ask many biologists.

"Open the map," says one of them. "Let's see where real, continuous taiga has been preserved. Trace it from south to north along the rivers. . . . The Kika and Turka—practically everything along the valleys has been burned or felled. . . . The Barguzin and Ina—clearcut. . . . This large stream—the same. . . . The Kabania—still a bit left. . . . The Shagnanda, Tompuda, Lower Angara—in spots somewhat intact. . . . The Kichekas and on the other, the left, bank . . . the Tyia, Rel, the right and left Ulkan—almost nothing. . . . The Tangoda, Lena, Buguldeika, Vanai, and Chanchur—fires and clearcut almost everywhere. . . . The Manzurka and Goloustnaia—little islands left here and there . . ."

Even on the territory of the Barguzin Reserve, the tiny pine seedlings remaining are not cared for as they should be; the pines were cut down for commercial reasons.

With the construction of the Baikal-Amur Mainline [BAM], in the adjacent northern and northeastern districts of the Baikal area, the harm done by economic—and noneconomic—activity is increasing rapidly.

For some reason the Baikal Commission's conclusions did not deal with the threat of oil pollution of the lake created by the construction of BAM. The number of ships carrying loads for the mainline is increasing constantly, and all Baikal ports are significantly expanding. Gasoline, diesel fuel, grease, and other petroleum products from every settlement's workshops, garages, and railroad car depots gather drop by drop, trickle by trickle, stream by stream into a constant, black petroleum tributary of Baikal.

Altogether the commission urged the prompt institution of a series of protective measures that would cost more than all the purifying equipment and conservation measures carried out at Lake Baikal since 1964. But the members of the commission and G. I. Galazii, whose institute has until now selflessly defended the lake, have not concealed their skepticism regarding the government's largesse.

However, Baikal has now become too well known as an ecological problem, too urgent a political issue for people to acquiesce in its obvious destruction. Of course some funds will be released, mainly for cosmetic, superficially effective, but palliative measures. Something will be given, but not too much, since at the very moment the right hand of the Ministry of Finances is reluctantly dispensing a few thousand for the preservation of Baikal, its left hand doles out tens of millions for the construction of an industrial complex at the extreme north of the lake, on the Kholodnaia River, just forty kilometers from its shores.

For more than fifteen years public attention has been focused on the southern part of Baikal; not long ago, for example, the construction of a closed water-circulating system at the Selenginskii paper and pulp combine was ballyhooed as a great achievement: since with it (supposedly) the combine will not pollute the lake. Yet at the same time, plans were being drafted at secret institutes for the construction of lead and zinc mines, a concentrating mill, a thermoelectric station, and a large settlement with roads and other facilities on the Kholodnaia River.

Construction is now in full swing. The complex should be ready for operation by 1980. Sewage and atmospheric discharges from all the nonferrous metallurgy works are among the most ecologically harmful. Even after treatment they will undoubtedly do more harm to Baikal than the effluents from the BPPC. Compared to sewage waters containing heavy metals, the runoffs from the Baikal combine will probably seem like harmless fizzwater.

Lead and zinc are, of course, strategic raw materials. And so no one is allowed to ask how much the country needs specifically Baikal lead and zinc, or how much any lead and zinc at all are needed for our security.

The absurdity of contaminating Baikal with sewage from the BPPC, and now from the Kholodnaia combine, has its own quite sober justifications——the interests of military industrial production. But economics, morality, and common sense halt before the words "defensive, strategic interests" and the like. The pure, fresh waters of Lake Baikal have alone been estimated to be worth approximately five times the national income of the USSR.[5] It is difficult to determine what each ton of the Kholodnaia lead or zinc will cost, but it is obvious that whatever they might add to our military superpower will be at a price to us of irretrievable losses. Losses on the economic, on the ecological, and what is most important, on the moral level. Baikal has existed for twenty-five million years (Lake Ladoga or the American Great Lakes are only several thousand years old); it has survived a multitude of geological cataclysms, a multitude of changes in the animal and plant world. But the "antiquity" of Baikal cannot survive the social transformations that have taken place in *homo sapien's* world in just a few decades of the twentieth century.

So far not one line about the ecological threat of the Kholodnaia complex has percolated into the press. And we can assume that it will not trickle through until the complex opens. At least the lesson of the Baikal campaign of the sixties was not lost on the censor.

The last official declaration about Baikal, made at the Twenty-fifth Congress of the Communist Party, bears a strong resemblance to the empty statements by the planners of the Baikal combine at the end of the fifties. "The measures undertaken ensure not only the preservation but even the augmentation of the natural riches of the Baikal Basin and the lake itself. Comrades, we need not be concerned about the fate of Baikal. The Central Committee of the party and the Soviet government, the workers of the Trans-Baikal and the Baikal Region are assiduously watching over it," declared A. U. Modagoev, the first secretary of the Buryat Regional Committee, in a speech.[6]

Does this mean, then, that in 1980, after the Kholodnaia complex opens, Chivilikhin's "Goodbye Baikal!" can be said with good reason? It is difficult to pinpoint the exact date of the lake's demise. Such a tremendous body of water, so ancient and durable an organism as Baikal is not so easily nor so quickly ruined. The authors of the report of the last Baikal Commission of the Academy of Sciences came up with a very precise formulation of the continuing tragedy: "Baikal is not easy to pollute, but it will be impossible to clean up." In any case, Baikal will still be purer than other lakes during our generation's lifetime. It is difficult to say how clean, but epishura will clearly survive Zhavoronkov.

Major ecological problems in the Soviet Union began with Baikal, but unfortunately they will not end with the lake. During these years "the blue orb of Siberia" has become a symbol of hundreds of Russian lakes and rivers being ruined by pollution, a symbol of the smoke-filled sky suffocating forests and people, a symbol of perishing nature.

The tragedy that began on the banks of the "sacred sea" is currently unfolding—and often much more rapidly—on the banks of the Azov, the Neman, the Volga, and the Irtysh, in the mountains of the Caucasus and Urals. The second act of the Baikal tragedy encompasses vast regions in various parts of the country.

"Actually, we have already lost the Azov, the Aral, and probably the Caspian as well," said one of the top officials of the State Planning Committee in a private conversation.

What a game! Like a card player the State Planning Committee is paying for its economic and social losses with chunks of its former patrimony: with lakes, rivers, lands, and whole seas. (As if they were indeed the property of the bureaucrats of the State Planning Committee or the Council of Ministers!)

"The ecological crisis is steadily deepening in the capitalist countries, but in the USSR there are no signs of it." Such is the official viewpoint, reiterated time and again by the ideologues of the Central Committee of the Communist Party.[7]

So there is no crisis because signs of it have not received official recognition by the ideologues. And the struggle with the crisis is being waged across a good two thirds of the country with the same methods that ensure the preservation of Baikal—with the help of censorship. As the ecological situation worsened at the beginning of the seventies, special circulars restricting the scope of information on pollution were issued at least two times. Since 1975 you will not find a single reference to pollution of the air, the water, or the soil even in special articles. Only indirect, abstract figures are published that tell nothing about the kind of air we breathe, the kind of water we drink and swim in, assuming that we take salubrious sea baths in the Crimea or at the Caucasus coast . . .

The composition of the air, of our drinking and sea water is a state secret. These statistics are the property of the government, just like the earth, the rivers, and the forests and their denizens the animals.

A Soviet citizen can get a fully detailed, disastrous picture of the state of nature in the United States or the Federal Republic of Germany. He can read in Russian agitated and profound books by Commoner, Grzimek, Parsons, or Douglas. The poisoning of Lake Erie, the oil-drenched beaches of England, and the mountains of garbage in New York even flash before him on the television screen to convince him of the advantages of his own, socialist, way of life. In the West hundreds of books and articles come out, public opinion loudly protests the depredation of nature in the interests of capitalists, and——somehow ——the success of such protests mounts. The public's influence on the solution of ecological problems is becoming a very powerful factor. But as the Baikal story has shown, for us mass participation in solving such problems is practically impossible. One of the main reasons for this is the lack of objective information, the impossibility of comprehending the situation as a whole and its possible development.

The Soviet citizen must simply believe the statement that socialism itself, by its very essence, guarantees harmony between man and nature, that "universal ownership of the means of production and of all natural resources foreordains the successful resolution of ecological problems in the USSR."[8]

Too often, however, ecological problems in our country are dealt with on the "showcase principle," the showcase of the Soviet store that provides propaganda about "achievements" rather than information about what is in the store. It is an exhibition of specially made samples of goods turned out under unusual conditions that are meant to be taken for mass, common products.

The millions invested in reequipping the Shchekino Chemical Combine, which was polluting the forest of Tolstoy's Yasnaya Polyana, figure prominently in any book about the conservation of nature in the USSR. But what about the hundreds of other forests withering to the roots thanks to hundreds of other chemical and nonchemical combines? There is not enough money for them. But isn't that the reason foreigners don't show up there—what would interest them there? And our own people don't make a fuss, if not ordered to . . .

The Baikal treatment facilities impress foreigners; their favorable remarks are presented to the public as objective evidence that "everything is fine at Baikal." But why must we determine the welfare or woe of our own nature through the responses of foreigners who, of course, were not given the confidential figures on the state of the fauna in the lake or on the purity of its water, through the responses of visitors who came to our country "to have a good time" and not to carry out secret investigations?

Primitive Potemkin villages no longer fool anyone; but after having personally touched two or three excellent samples (which "just happened" to be on the Intourist itinerary), many Europeans and Third World visitors believe that they are experts on successful environmental protection in Russia. Especially genetically predisposed to the wiles of showcases are such people as the French Marxist Guy Biolat[9] or the Italian Communist Senator T. Budesto, who declared that only socialism and only the USSR could provide what was necessary for the preservation of nature.

Of course, the showcase does not influence merely foreigners. The Soviet citizen gets his basic ideas about the problems of the environment in the USSR by contemplating the same showcase on television or in the cinema, in the pages of newspapers and magazines. He can speculate about the negative side of the matter only on the basis "of a few critical facts."

On the other hand, experts on nature conservation speak (among themselves, of course) about a few positive facts and a multitude of extremely serious problems to which the authorities close their eyes, whose resolution is put off to "a higher stage of development of the country's economy," or even openly to the "communist future."

Of course there is an ecological crisis in the country, and this book is devoted entirely to it. And the ideologue K. Mitriushkin and others writing and speaking on the problems of preserving the environment are excellently informed about its worsening. There exist confidential studies by various institutes, and in the last few years the Hydrometeorological Service has begun to publish a regular *Bulletin of Environmental Pollution*, also confidential, of course. In it the panorama of ecological woes of the country are spelled out in real figures.

The notorious resolution of the Council of Ministers of the USSR (No. 898, December 29, 1972) on Intensifying the Preservation of Nature and Improving the Use of Natural Resources provided for making scientific forecasts of the state of the environment over the next twenty to thirty years. Such forecasts have been compiled by special commissions directed by such authoritative scholars as Academicians Gerasimov, Fedorenko, and the head of the Hydrometeorological Service, Corresponding Member of the Academy of Sciences Izrael.

But even these statistics are accessible to only a narrow circle of experts who are bound by their signatures not to divulge official information. Secretiveness is the best indicator that the environmental situation in the country is serious. That the ecological crisis has gone so far that information about the actual situation would damage the authority of the government within the country and the prestige of the socialist state in the international arena.

Forecasts about the state of nature in 1980 and 1990 paint a far from rosy perspective. Indeed, the situation is even worse, since neither these forecasts nor other alarming materials lying in the safes of the State Planning Committee have had any major influence on the course of development of the economy.

The ecological crisis has now assumed global dimensions. But on what scale is it going on in our country? What characterizes our relationship with a dying nature? What are the alternatives?

Without disparaging either the difficult work of biologists and engineers or the splendid achievements of our talented and noble countrymen (achievements that have borne their fruits despite everything), in this book we will discuss only one side of the matter—the ravaging of nature, the systematic devastation of Russian, Kazakh, Estonian, Ukrainian nature . . . what prompts it, who benefits from the ruination, who is indifferent, and who bears the losses.[10]

It is our conviction that the ecological alarm in our country, a country with an inflexible economy, government, and ideology, cannot be too loud nor too premature.

Profoundly apt for the country as a whole are the words of the scientists about Baikal: "It is easy to pollute, but it will be impossible to clean up later."

# 2 Secret Air

*"What color is snow?" Ilya Repin was once asked. "Just not white, just not white," bristled the old man.*

Today almost any city dweller would readily agree with this somewhat odd assertion by the great realist. In Leningrad, Moscow, and the large cities of the Urals and Siberia, the snow is actually white so rarely that it is hard to catch a glimpse of it that way. Quite soon it becomes black from coal, gray from cement, and dark brown from other dusts.

At the end of 1977 something new was noted in the capital: the snow fell to earth already black. Somewhere in the heavens the snow crystals had stuck to flakes of soot. . .

On the Kola Peninsula, in an area of superphosphate plants, after the snow melts the entire winter's dust covers the grass and lichen in such a thick layer that it blocks photosynthesis and the plants die if a heavy rain does not wash the dirt from them.

In the center of industrial Zaporozhe or Dneprodzerzhinsk it is as difficult to "catch" the snow while it is white as it is to find greenery green. The windows of buildings and houses located there are tightly closed the year round.

"You're from the State Planning Committee?" the employees of one organization asked the visitor. "Your bosses should be here to get their eyes eaten away like ours!"

One can cite the example of a Ural city where a special workers' brigade was created to clean away the dirt and soot accumulated on roofs every three months. Otherwise the roofs would collapse. Or another city where window panes are replaced much more frequently than anywhere else, since they quickly become thin and brittle from the acid in the air.

What is a Soviet citizen breathing as he watches with a sense of superiority a TV program about the suffocating Los Angeles smog? He can judge the pollutedness of his own air only by eye, depending on the sensitivity of his lungs and bronchia.

*The Bulletin on the Problems of Environmental Pollution*, published for a narrow circle of specialists and ministry workers, assesses in very general form the situation in the country as follows:

Cities with an average level of noxious gases in the atmosphere of 100 MPCs—about 10;

Cities with an average level of noxious gases in the atmosphere of 10 MPCs—about 100;

Cities with an average level of noxious gases in the atmosphere of 5 MPCs—over 1,000.[1]

But what is the MPC? Are 100 MPCs or 10 MPCs a lot or a little? Is it worth getting excited about? What does "maximum permissible concentration" mean; is it a maximum limit of pollution safe for health if it can be exceeded 100 times?

The Soviet Union has the strictest standards in the world for many pollutants. And they were adopted earlier than in all the major countries of the West; however, these strict MPCs have generally remained an abstraction, an ideal for which industry should strive. Or as the theoreticians say, "approach gradually" from one five-year plan to another.

What dangers do the different levels of atmospheric pollution pose for human beings?

There is a simple table that illustrates this danger.

According to this table a concentration of material up to 5 MPCs is considered a warning zone.

A concentration of 10 to 15 MPCs is a zone of immediate threat to health.

A concentration of 25 MPCs and above is a zone of extreme hazard to health.

Extreme hazard means that constant presence in such a zone for weeks and months endangers not only your health but the health of your progeny. Experiments with white mice, carried out at the institute of the M. Pinigin Clean Air Laboratory, show that after 500 hours in an atmosphere containing 20 MPCs of sulfur dioxide, the sex cells of these mice suffered irreversible changes.

Of all the ways for toxic substances to get into our body, the respiratory pathway is the most dangerous. We also take in a considerable amount of polymers and other dirt with our food and water, but our alimentary tract and kidneys contain organisms that break down these generally long and complicated molecules into smaller fragments, in which form they are eliminated from the body. Geochemically diverse regions and areas of the continents differ appreciably from one another, and the human organism has more or less adapted to this. But the composition of the air has been the same everywhere for hundreds and thousands of years, so that nature has not provided analogous defense mechanisms in the lungs and bronchia.

This explains to some extent the fact that approximately 68 percent of the harm done to the population by environmental pollution comes from illnesses brought about by inhaling polluted air: from cancer of the lungs to sterility.

Official reports say that the greatest pollution has been observed for many years in those cities that are centers for nonferrous and ferrous metallurgy and the chemical industry.

"The acknowledged leader" on these black lists is Leninogorsk (Eastern Kazakhstan). The almost 100,000 inhabitants of this city breathe air containing average levels of 30 to 40 MPCs of lead, and on some days this concentration has risen to 440 MPCs!

In neighboring Ust-Kamenogorsk (Eastern Kazakhstan; 270,000 inhabitants) the lead concentrations are 14 times the maximum permissible level, and here too often rise to 100 MPCs.

In a third Kazakhstan center for nonferrous metallurgy, Temir-Tau, the mercury concentrations in the air exceed the norm by 60 times.

Chemists in Sterlitamak (Bashkiria) breathe easily compared with Temir-Tau: there the mercury level is only 10 MPCs, although to be sure the mercury vapors are accompanied by carbon monoxide 21 times the norm and chlorine 17 times the norm.

The Omsk "bouquet" also features carbon monoxide (20 MPCs) and a selection of a number of other gases at 10 MPCs and higher.

In Krivoi Rog, a famous center of the iron ore industry, enormous sulfur dioxide ($SO_2$) concentrations, up to 100 MPCs, are common.

In Erevan, located in a mountain trough, the chemical and nonferrous metallurgy industries have been booming in recent years. As a result the air of the capital of Armenia contains on the average 21 times the MPC of carbon monoxide, 7 times the

MPC of sulfur dioxide, as well as dangerous levels of phenol, fluorine, and hydrogen.

Often our sense of smell or our other senses do not give us any signals about dangerous pollution with chemical compounds. Special instruments are found in observatories to which neither the press nor the public have access without permission from the authorities.

Hence the struggle for clean air often becomes a battle against smoke. Factories spend money mainly on filters that trap ash particles and disperse the black smoke puffs above smokestacks. "There is clean air over our combine," the press accurately informs the public. However, although the filters catch the large particles, they let through invisible nitrogen and sulfur oxides that had been bound in ash particles. But now these oxides enter the atmosphere in pure form and are more easily dissolved by rain drops, and the harm done by pollution with such rain drops actually increases. Above our smokestacks actually hangs a pure, shimmering mirage.

At a giant cement plant on the shores of the Black Sea at Novorossiisk, some expensive filters were installed, and the clouds of dust that used to shroud the entire city have almost disappeared. But half of this cleanup is an optical illusion. The filters do not retain the tiny, invisible particles, and in a fair wind they fly across the bay onto inhabited areas. Yet this very fine dust is the most dangerous for the lungs.

The situation is similar in Bratsk. No thick smoke can be seen over the city. The files of the local Intourist office are full of compliments to the young Siberian city. But the instruments record levels of CO, $SO_2$, ammonia, and other gases many times exceeding the norms. Forestry experts have sounded the alarm ——the taiga around Bratsk, to say nothing of the green areas within the town limits, is rapidly withering. One hundred per-cent of the seedlings are dying.

In addition to Bratsk and Temir-Tau, other cities, such as Novokuznetsk, Amursk, and Magnitogorsk, also have dangerous and extremely dangerous levels of pollution. Almost all of them are former Komsomol projects. For three decades these names ——Magnitka, Kuznetsk, etc.——were equated with the idea of "a bright future" in glowing articles in periodicals. Completed now, these cities evoke quite different associations.

Mayakovsky's celebrated lines about Kuznetsk (now called Novokuznetsk, for a while Stalinsk)——"I know a city will exist, I know a garden will bloom, when such people exist in the Soviet land"——are heard less and less. "There was no garden," affirms Chivilikhin, speaking of Novokuznetsk. "There were poplars on a few streets, but they were chopped down because of the allergenic pollen, although they could simply have been pruned. . . ."

In the most famous Komsomol city, Komsomolsk-on-Amur, the air is relatively clean and there is much greenery. But in its satellite Amursk, built in the sixties, a huge paper and pulp combine operates. (The press wrote nothing about its construction and the ecological danger it posed. There was no Baikal as yet.) The effluents from the combine transformed the huge lake into a noisome cesspool; and the oppressive odor often carries as far as the Trans-Siberian Railroad, forcing passengers to hold their noses, and even to Komsomolsk, located forty kilometers away.

In early 1977, at one of the sessions of the USSR State Planning Committee, the record levels of lung cancer and other diseases of the respiratory tract in the Novokuznetsk and Kemerovo industrial regions were discussed. The first-born of socialist industry proved to be new smoky Manchesters and Pittsburghs from the early twentieth century. Was this an accident?

The "first-born" were built during the first difficult five-year plans, when there was no such thing as ecology. Let us assume. Such now smoky cities as Norilsk were built by prisoners even during the war. No questions here either. But Rustavi and the other Georgian center for metallurgy, Zestafoni, Chimkent and Zhdanov, and the recent Sterlitamak——they were projects from the end of the fifties and sixties. Why stint on environmental preservation there?

And finally, Tynda, the capital of the Baikal-Amur Mainline, where smog has already begun to hang over the streets, when the city and industrial conglomerate are not even half built. Couldn't ecological factors have been considered immediately? . . . If they had wanted to consider them . . .

Photos of prerevolutionary Yuzovka in school books on the history of the USSR provide a graphic idea of capitalist predators who spit on the workers, on nature, on everything except profits.

Contemporary Donetsk is renowned for the greenery on its streets and the cleanness of its air. The local botanical garden has raised dozens of splendid varieties of flowers and shrubbery resistant to environmental pollution. They brighten the area around many factories and mines.

But the statistics in the confidential reports lack floral borders: morbidity from lung cancer among the population at large in Donetsk (not miners) is 300 percent higher than among the inhabitants of other cities. After this don't the flowers on the broad municipal lawns seem like modest daisies over graves? . . .

Shrubs and flowers cannot compensate for the high gas levels in many areas of the Ukraine. Plantings do not solve a single serious health problem in the industrial cities. On the other hand, the psychological effect of lawns and public gardens is considerable. What figure on the decrease in the phenol or sulfur dioxide concentration (if indeed it ever got into the press) could ever measure up in impression created to a simple blossom of camomile? To its vivid photo on a magazine cover?

Planting industrial zones is not an easy matter, but it is often easier to alter the biological constitution of plants and force them to bloom in a smokestack than to change a bureaucratic system that defends nature mainly with resolutions on paper.

". . . as the nation's economy continues to develop through 1990, atmospheric pollution may maintain, and in some cases exceed, levels extremely hazardous for health in some industrial centers of the USSR." This quotation is from a forecast of the state of the environment by 1990. In it, as in the forecast *Nature 1980*, some figures are cited on diseases linked to atmospheric pollution.

In the last decade the incidence of lung cancer has doubled in the USSR. Each year 5 to 6 percent more children are born with genetic defects than in the previous year, and the number of birth traumas and abortions is increasing at a rate of 6 to 7 percent a year. On the whole the rate of genetic defects among the population, i.e., the number of people who are genetically handicapped, is today 7 to 8 percent according to the statistics of Academician Dubinin, and at today's growth rates this could reach 15 percent by 1990.[2] In other words, in the upcoming generation almost every sixth adult will have some physical or mental debility. The question of genetic health remains especially acute, since in all the republics only the populations of Central Asia and Azerbaijan are increasing.

Each year the number of disabled children cared for by the state increases by 200,000, with the cost of their upkeep rising by approximately 120 million rubles per year. The total loss to the nation's economy due to pollution of the air and water (forecasts do not include losses due to pollution of the soil, since there are no reliable methods for estimating it) is estimated by experts to be 20 billion rubles, i.e., 5 percent of the national income by 1980. In the next ten years it will increase to 45 billion rubles, according to these estimates; according to data not included in the reports, by 1980 it could reach 50 to 60 billion rubles, and 120 billion rubles by 1990.[3] Almost half of these costs will be in the area of public health, while only 20 percent will be in agriculture and 12 percent in industry.

Although in the next few years industrial discharges into the atmosphere should be reduced, vehicular pollution will rapidly grow, and overall air pollution by 1980, according to forecasts, will have increased by 10 to 15 percent compared with 1975.

By 1990 it may have grown by almost 100 percent, with the automobile responsible for almost 70 percent (or a total of 242 million tons, with 172 million tons yearly due to the automobile).

Large cities suffer most, of course, from vehicular pollution. On the Nevskii Prospekt and other main streets of Leningrad, the nitrogen dioxide content some days reaches 50 MPCs and never falls below 5 MPCs.

There are not so many automobiles in the city—only 670,000; but it is not much easier to breathe even at some distance from the main highways. One Kirov factory emits 42 tons of pure carbon per day, and the CO content over the entire surrounding region is 15 to 25 times the norm. In areas adjacent to the Bolshevik and Plastpolimer factories, the concentrations of phenol and hydrogen sulfide remain at a level of 8 to 10 MPCs. Seventy percent of all the industrial enterprises in the city do not have dust traps. Hundreds of plants emit dozens of tons of dust per day, hundreds of plant managers pay fines every year (from their own pockets!), but air pollution continues to grow.

Today's air over "putrid Petrograd" contains about thirty chemically active impurities. This "bouquet" consists of aldehydes, esters, toluene, chromium vapors and alkalis, formaldehydes, and manganese (in addition to ordinary carbon monoxide and sulfur dioxide, phenol, and hydrogen sulfide).

Huge amounts of sulfur dioxide are emitted in Leningrad and in other cities by thermoelectric power and heating plants consuming coal and mazut. There is not one city of a million inhabitants that, in the forecast *Nature 1980*, would not rank among the cities with highly dangerous levels of sulfur dioxide pollution. In addition to our cities of one million inhabitants, industrial cities such as Riazan, Bereznika, Ufa, Dzerzhinsk, Angarsk, Novokuibyshevsk, Voronezh, and Dneprodzerzhinsk,

L. I. Brezhnev's native city, are also extremely polluted by the emissions from thermoelectric power plants.

However, it is not just the inhabitants of industrial regions who suffer from bad air. Bounteous nature, "rural calm" are becoming a myth before our eyes. The meanderings of unspoiled rivers, the sonorous silence and the soft contours of rolling hills evoking ancient town fortresses—all this is being destroyed or at best cluttered with pipelines, watertowers, and hulking factories. Along with the disrupted natural environment, a culture, too, going back five, even six centuries, is receding into the past.

The factories appearing in provincial cities are not as huge as their counterparts in the capitals. But the smaller the volume of production, the more costly is the treatment equipment and the adaptation of technology to the requirements of ecology. Still there are not many people in a small city, so that expenditures on health care are not so high.

Iuzhno-Sakhalinsk is a small city by our standards. and it is a seaside town. Nonetheless 200 days a year its air contains carbon monoxide ten times higher than the norm. And just as much phenol, sulfur dioxide, and soot. Sometimes the wind carries an odor from neighboring Dolinsk, where there is a paper and pulp combine.

The inhabitants of Volzhsk (near Volgograd) refuse to ride on trolleys and buses used by the workers from the methylcaprolactam plant. Trace amounts of this substance are added to natural gas so that people can smell leaks. A single molecule of methylcaprolactam per cubic meter of air irritates our sense of smell beyond the norm. The workers take this unpleasant odor home on their clothing, and not only passers-by but their wives and children as well avoid them. Reason, the force of habit —all are powerless before this smell. According to local vital statistics, the number of divorces doubled after this factory opened.

Okha and Korsaka on Sakhalin, Monchegorsk, Nikel, and Kola on the Kola Peninsula, Kunda in Estonia, Kingisepp and Pikalevo, Gatchina and Kirishi in Leningrad Province, Orsk, Troitsk, and Miass in the southern Urals, Sibai and Buribai in Bashkiria, Siberian Balakovo and Achinsk, Volga Komyshin, Novocherkassk and Nevinnomyssk in the northern Caucasus, Engels, Berdiansk, Kovrov, and Kolomna, Gurev and Staryi Oskol—the year round the air in these provincial cities contains 20 to 25 MPCs of various gases.

"We were born to make a fairy tale a reality . . ."—this is

no place to debate whether this poetic slogan has been turned into reality. But it is the place to say that a former reality——the fresh air of small cities throughout the country——has been transformed by the development of socialist industry into an old wive's tale.

The report *Nature 1980* says nothing about the air in the countryside. On the whole it is probably still clean; but medical studies say that in the Leningrad and Moscow areas the peasants get cancer as often as workers in the mines and pits. The dust from mineral fertilizers and pesticides, which are often sprayed from airplanes,[4] is inhaled in large quantities by the rural inhabitants, and these substances can have a very injurious effect even on human sex cells. Despite the generally poor chemical and equipment supply to agriculture, in this regard our collective farms are not too far behind superindustrialized American farms. In bounteous California, for example, farming as an occupation is ranked officially as most harmful to the health.[5]

The next myth is that the air of Moscow is clean and healthful.

Unquestionably, the atmosphere of the capital is cleaner than that in Leningrad, Tashkent, or Erevan, to say nothing of our metallurgical centers. However, on the whole the purity of Moscow air is a great myth produced by the newspapers, radio, and other organs of the mass media, just as giant Gargantua once sprung from the left ear of his mother Gargamelle.

Never has any panegyrist of the air of our capital presented any concrete data describing this purity in figures. It is obvious that this would demolish all propaganda efforts. The carbon monoxide content in Moscow's air in recent years has constantly exceeded ten to thirteen times the average daily MPC! In the Proletarsk, Perov, and Leningrad districts and on some main arteries in the city, the CO concentration rises to 20 to 24 MPCs. (It should be recalled that in the classification of Soviet health experts, 10 to 15 MPCs is a zone of immediate danger, while 25 MPCs and above means extreme danger to health.)

The hydrogen sulfide content in the air exceeds the norm for six months out of the year. Sometimes its concentration reaches 7 to 8 MPCs. Sulfur dioxide, dust, nitrogen dioxide, and phenol all, although infrequently, exceed the norms by five and even ten and nineteen times. The newspapers parade the figures: 470 industrial enterprises and 180 garages are equipped with complete air- and water-treatment systems——but that almost as many Moscow plants and factories are not equipped with such systems they mute.

It is an old journalistic trick to wittingly compare different things to prove what one wants. The air of Moscow is compared with the air of Los Angeles, New York, or Tokyo, where there are ten to fifteen times more cars than in Moscow. On this basis it is concluded that Moscow has the cleanest air of all the major cities in the world. The list never includes Washington, London, or Stockholm, where, although there are more cars, people breathe more easily. And if the number of cars is left out of account, then the cleanest air is in Peking!

The important point is that since 1974-75, exhaust gas pollution has begun to decrease somewhat in Western capitals and in Tokyo, while in Moscow it is on the rise.

According to newspaper propaganda, the air of Soviet cities is becoming cleaner and cleaner; yet according to the data of the forecasts in *Nature 1980* and other sources, it is getting worse.

M. Ia. Lemeshev, a well-known economist who deals with problems of ecology, once declared that our economy cannot afford to spend 15 to 20 percent of the cost of each plant or factory on preserving the environment.[6]

According to Lemeshev, the installation of a filter on automobile exhaust pipes that would substantially decrease automobile exhaust fumes in city air would also be an inadmissible luxury for us. Such a filter, which is now installed on every Swedish automobile (as a result of which the air of Stockholm and other Swedish cities has significantly cleared), increases the cost of an automobile by about 15 percent. The retail prices of our small cars are already increasing by the same percentage almost every year, yet our economy cannot afford to increase the net cost of a Zhiguli or a Moskvich by 15 percent . . . But in five to ten years labor productivity will have increased, and then perhaps . . .

The notion that we have a great deal of time to correct the situation before it reaches the point of Los Angeles's smog is another myth. Propaganda illusions are easily dispelled by comparing them with real figures.

How much worse is the situation with the "capitalists"? Sample figures indicate a modest gap. The CO quantity in the air of large U.S. cities at peak hours reaches 30 to 40 of our MPCs. Concentrations of 20-30 MPCs are no rarity on the streets of our Leningrad, Moscow, Baku, Tashkent, and Novosibirsk.

Even 40 and 50 MPCs occur. Can we really boast that there is less poison on our highways than they have if we already have quite enough to ruin people's health?

The absolute figures are much more important in this case, and they show approximately the same picture. The forecast *Nature 1980* says that each year in our country about 110 million tons of various pollutants are pumped into the "dump above." (The forecast cites the figure of 95 million tons for 1975 and 114 million tons for 1980 owing to an increase in the number of automobiles. Experts say that both figures are at least 10 percent too low. However, let's stick to the official figures.)

Thus in the USSR there are 110 million tons, and in the United States, 130 million tons. The Soviet Union is almost three times the area of the United States excluding Alaska, but the densely populated part of the USSR is commensurate with the United States.

Most of the pollution, of course, affects the inhabitants of large cities and urban industrial agglomerations. In the Soviet Union about 140 million people live in such agglomerations, while in the United States there are roughly 170 million. This means that 55 to 60 percent of our population must breathe almost the same bad air (only one fifth better) as the majority of Americans.

Development trends indicate that by 1982-84, almost our entire country will be breathing air that will be somewhat worse than the air today in U.S. cities. In the United States there is a growing trend toward decreasing air pollution from exhaust fumes.

Today, having polluted their atmospheric ocean 15 to 18 percent more than we have ours, the United States produces more than twice more than the USSR. Americans now have 5.5 times more automobiles than we do (in the United States there are 110 million cars; in the USSR there are 18 to 20 million), but they pollute the atmosphere only 1.4 times more. In other words, for each unit of goods the socialist economy produces twice as many air pollutants of all sorts, and each Soviet automobile poisons its environment almost four times as much as each American car. (The difference is explained by the more intensive use of cars in the Soviet Union and poorer engine control.)

Our scientists are at the international level in the development of ecologically clean motors. However, if even tomorrow a splendid hydrogen or other clean motor were built in the USSR,

how many years would it take for the Soviet automobile indus-
try to put it into mass production? . . . The experts say that the
question must be put another way: how many decades? . . .

Such are the facts in the light of real figures. They provide
no cause for optimism; on the contrary, they force us to ponder
not only clean air but also the methods of current socialist man-
agement of the economy. The facts do not provide us hope for
cleaner air in our cities, nor even for a reduction in the present
rates of increase of air pollution.

# 3 Secret Water

In 1966 a Swedish bilogist discovered in Baltic fish and later in the body and feathers of an eagle a very dangerous compound—polychlorinated biphenyls. The world had learned of a new enemy—PCB.

PCB had been synthesized as early as the thirties by American chemists, but after the Swedish discovery interest in PCB grew sharply. It was soon found that PCB was present in practically all living organisms along with DDT, and even more frequently: in the seals of the Arctic and the penguins of Antarctica.

In 1969 some PCB leaked out of cooling systems into rice oil, and thousands of Japanese became seriously ill. The PCB content in Lake Michigan salmon exceeded five parts per billion, and their use as food was prohibited. "Nonetheless," writes the well-known ecologist Barry Commoner, "PCB was a basic ingredient in the breakfasts of Americans, since various packaging materials containing PCB were widely used until 1970 to pack products."[1]

An excellent plasticizer, PCB was also added to insulating materials and used in the production of expensive paints, high-grade pastes for ballpoint pens, and copying paper. Sooner or later these materials ended up in the dump and were burned; however, PCB molecules possess a phenomenal stability and are affected by neither heat nor cold. They evaporated intact with the smoke and later returned to earth and the ocean with rain drops.

A negligible quantity of PCB profoundly disrupts the reproduction of fish, birds, and mammals. Even as little as 0.0000005 grams per liter of water is capable of transforming an entire ocean into a wasteland. The waters of the North Atlantic now contain 0.000000035 grams per liter at the surface and 0.00000001 grams at a depth of 200 meters. This is just one order of magnitude below a lethal dose.

The production of PCB has been halted almost everywhere, and its use has come under strict control.

After the International Convention on the Prevention of Pollution in the Baltic was signed on March 6, 1974, in Helsinki, Swedish vessels began to make spot checks for PCB along their own as well as the Soviet coast. The data indicated large concentrations, which were increasing especially at the mouth of the Neman and other rivers.

Between 1974 and 1976 the Swedes requested several times that prompt measures be taken. The Soviets declared that PCB was not produced in the USSR nor would it be. There was no reason to take steps.

The Swedes insisted.

"But where would we get PCB?" asked Soviet experts, honestly bewildered. "It is in high-grade paints, copying paper, ballpoint pens. But as everyone knows, for heaven's sakes, our pens don't write, the paints are terrible, copying paper is even worse. Everything is okay over here! You'd better check your instruments."

The Swedes checked—PCB was flowing out of the Neman.

"Check them again. We don't have such instruments, but it's possible that PCB gets here in the rain from the West. No one ever heard of PCB in the USSR."

Finally, in the summer of 1976 a woman working at the Institute for Applied Geophysics of the Hydrometeorological Service began a few control measurements, and PCB was found in literally every body of water in the Soviet Union! In Baikal, in Ladoga, in all the rivers, and, of course, in the Neman.

The Soviet specialists, particularly the experts from the Sysin Institute of Health, were absolutely sincere when they denied that anything was known about PCB in our country. In accordance with the existing rules, the Sysin Institute should have been notified about all new pollutants that any enterprise at any point in the country released into the environment. And it knew nothing. The secret of PCB, as might have been expected, was buried in one of the defense ministries. Since the fifties PCB had been produced in Dzerzhinsk near Gorky for extrastrong insulation for military equipment. Later it began to be produced at other sites; but appropriate precautionary measures were not taken, and the health experts were not informed, either inadvertently or for reasons of secrecy.

The Sysin Institute of Communal Health is an institution of international repute, and if Soviet scientists had learned in time about PCB, they would have perceived the danger and told the world about it long before the discoveries of the Swedish biologist. The PCB level in Baikal, in our drinking water and in our food products, and hence in our blood, would then have been much lower. However, here too "strategic interests" prevailed. In the most literal sense strategic interests pervade our whole being whether we want them or not.

(Unfortunately, a page was missing from the manuscript, so we must leave a gap here. The editors.)

Anyone who watches television has a good idea of the shape of the treatment facilities at the petrochemical combine in Kirishi on the Volkhov River. They have been shown countless times in various films and broadcasts about preserving nature. The facilities at Kirishi are impressive: huge round concrete basin-ponds —in some the sewage is purified by bacteria; in others the water is saturated with oxygen, jets of which prettily rise from the bottom. The water is returned to the river clean and clear. It really is that way. But according to Barry Commoner, it is just such waters that destroyed Lake Erie. ". . . sewage treatment will convert nearly all (about 90 percent) of the organic matter originally present in the raw sewage into inorganic products . . . to nitrates and phosphates . . . but in Lake Erie a large part of these compounds serve as nutritive material for a tremendous proliferation of algae, i.e., they are again transformed into organic material which requires a huge amount of oxygen, and this has had a catastrophic effect on the biology of the lake." ". . . in many areas, the lake is literally the appearance and consistency of pea soup."[2]

The cold climate and the hydrological characteristics of the Baltic might slow down processes of eutrophication—overfertilization with nitrates—but they cannot alter the direction of the process.

A new system of treatment, i.e., trapping phosphates and nitrates in purifying equipment, might change it. But so far our industry has counted on old systems used by the Americans in the fifties and sixties, which led to such sad results at Lakes Erie, Michigan, and other places. The multimillion-ruble facilities on the Volga and in the Urals, which are being installed after the special resolution on stopping pollution of the Volga and Ural basins, will also operate in the old way, pouring millions of tons of nitrites and phosphates into the rivers.

Engineers concerned with the problems of treatment still don't want to give up the idea that current treatment systems will handle the situation if they are made a little larger. In 1976 and 1977, at various conferences, it was necessary to demonstrate to specialists from academic institutes, to convince them that the threat of secondary pollution was quite serious. Data had to be presented showing that despite the tens of millions of rubles invested, Volga water has not become better (although it is no longer getting worse), and that there is almost no hope of returning to Mother Volga its purity.

The campaign by the Americans to save Lake Erie has serious underpinnings, particularly since they can now extract phosphates not only from the sewage but from Erie itself. Our research on secondary pollution is proceeding very slowly. We do not have the means. In any event, there has been progress in philology—since 1976 the term "eutrophication" has been spelled Western style.

In addition to the industrial waste waters, a considerable quantity of nitrites and phosphates enters the seas and lakes with agricultural wastes.

Today in the USSR more mineral fertilizers are produced than in all other countries, but more of them is leached from the fields than in any other country as well: on the average 80 percent of the fertilizer applied. In Estonia this figure has reached 90 percent.

It is agricultural rather than industrial wastes which threaten to contaminate the Armenian Lake Sevan, which will never recover from the damage done by the hydroelectric plants at Sevan Falls.

Every year some percentage of fertilizers and soil particles is unavoidably eroded from fields. In the United States, for example, the leaching of mineral fertilizer is estimated at 36 percent, while in Japan it is 20 percent of the total applied. Here a large number of mineral fertilizer plants process noxious blue-green algae supplements.

When at some conference the representatives of the Ministry of Agriculture have been asked what they are doing to stop pollution of the environment, they have answered that many new storage sites for fertilizer and pesticides will be constructed in the next five-year period, so that they will not be carried away by the rivers before they even get to the fields . . . the Ministry of Agriculture could not even consider anything more.

Nonetheless more dangerous substances than fertilizers are flowing into the rivers: DDT and the veterinary preparations POS (phosphorus-organic substances) and HCH (hexachlorcyclo-hexan). A good portion of these substances is lost due to un-tutored use and negligence. According to some data, the waters of the Dniepr, the Dniestr, and the Prut contain 2 to 4 MPCs of POS and HCH the year round.

In Kirghizia, with its livestock industry, practically all open bodies of water contain 4 to 6 MPCs of these compounds, and in the resort area of Lake Issyk-Kul the level is 2 to 3 MPCs. According to statistics from the Ministry of Agriculture, about 100,000 tons of pesticides, defoliants, and other poisonous chemicals are used each year in Uzbekistan alone. In this respect Uzbekistan is first in the country; it is not surprising that DDT and other dangerous substances have been found there, for the first time in the USSR, in concentrations above the MPC in the ground water of whole regions. The experts write with trepida-tion about supplying the population with clean water in the nearest future.

Oil, too, is flowing from the fields into the rivers. There is no sector of the economy that spills as much gasoline, diesel fuel, and grease as the collective farms and state farms, where they are constantly in short supply. Even now the fleets of farm machines are washed mainly in rivers and streams, just as horses once were bathed.

The Soviet press writes absolutely nothing about oil pollu-tion. One of the rare publications—an article by Oleg Zeinalov in the *Baku Worker* of June 21, 1974—reflects only a fragment of the vast panorama. Oil production near Baku flooded a huge lake with oil and killed tens of thousands of birds wintering there. The organization responsible paid the Azerbaijan Conser-vation Committee 100,000 rubles, but this sum reflected neither the actual damage done nor the prospective costs of restoring the decimated bird flocks to their former numbers (if anyone even tried).

Reading Soviet newspapers one could get the impression that oil spills into the sea are a privilege of Western countries. Each instance of a catastrophe with one of "their" tankers or mile-long oil slicks on "their" coasts is broadcast by our tele-vision as a dose of tranquilizer: "Look, viewer, we don't have the outrages they do."

As for our own problems, it is mainly reported that the strictest laws have been passed against the pollution of seas and rivers. For example, in Azerbaijan only the chairman of the council of ministers of the republic can approve releasing oil from the pipes of off-shore wells, and, of course, only in an emergency situation. In practical terms, if the threat of oil rupturing pipes occurs, the drillers face many problems, including loss of part of their pay; so the foreman quietly orders the oil poured into the sea. Such cases are never recorded anywhere, and hence it is believed that no oil has gotten into the water.

Around Baku the oil concentration along the entire seashore never goes below 20 MPCs. Along 200 kilometers of beach it is difficult to find a place where there are no black globs of mazut on the sand or rainbow-colored films on the water.

At the Caspian Sea oil is extracted, while on the Baltic and at Klaipeda it is only processed; yet in the Neman estuary oil concentrations reach 30 and at times 60 MPCs. The midstream oil concentration in the Volga is 25 to 30 MPCs, and in the Don it is even higher—51 MPCs.

According to the forecast *Nature 1980*, the entire resort area along the Black Sea from Odessa to Batumi is highly polluted with oil. In all regions—Kherson, Yalta, Sevastopol, Gelendzhik, Tuapse, Pitsunda, and Sukhumi—the coastal waters contain 10 to 12 MPCs of oil. And in addition there is about the same level of phenol. Bacterial contamination has also reached dangerous levels at most resorts.

One of the most complex scientific problems on which experts at the Sysin Institute of Health are working is setting standards for sea water suitable for swimming. The standard is for a permissible amount of chemicals that will cause no harm if it sometimes gets in the mouth or is absorbed through the skin. There is no longer any point in referring to benefits from sea baths; the important thing is that swimming in the Black Sea should not be harmful! It's no joke anymore!

Quite apart from the hazard it poses for bathers, oil destroys communities of marine organisms. Studies by Professor Mironov from the Odessa Institute of Marine Biology paint a gloomy picture.

According to his calculations marine colonies along the Soviet coast of the Black Sea are capable of decomposing up to 2,000 tons of oil per year—approximately two tons for every kilometer of shore line. The degradation of marine organisms would not be too great in this case. However, our rivers alone dump about 100,000 tons of oil each year into the sea . . .

According to Mironov's report, oil pollution also is a hazard because some petroleum fractions get into sediments and later can again pollute surface layers.

Odessa scientists demonstrated that the roe and fry of the Black Sea gray mullet die at concentrations one tenth of the permissible norms of oil. If young are nonetheless spawned from these eggs, their bodies are twisted into a spiral. The poor things cannot straighten out and soon die.

Methods for treating sea water using special strains of bacteria that feed on oil are still in the experimental stage. Soviet experts use chemicals very sparingly. Hence the rate at which oil in the sea is dispersed depends primarily on weather, wind, and air temperature. At a temperature below 5°C oil floats for years on the surface of our northern seas.

In the small Sea of Azov the level of oil pollution is many times higher even than in the Black Sea. Water samples taken from it often contain 100 MPCs. In addition phenol and zinc are also present in huge quantities: 40 to 50 MPCs. At one time famed for its fantastic catches of sturgeon, carp, and perch, Azov has become a latrine, as it were, for the industrial south of Russia and the Ukraine.

The oxygen deficit in the water causes mass asphyxiation and death of fish shoals that somehow had tolerated the dissolved zinc, phenol, and oil. According to the forecast *Nature 1980* the catch in Azov is currently about 3,000 tons of fish. This represents about one ninetieth of what was taken there in the postwar period. The small Sea of Azov, warmed by the sun, modestly saline, was the most productive body of water in the world. It yielded three times the fish of the Black Sea, the Caspian, and the Baltic together! It could actually supply 1.5 kilograms of sturgeon, pike, or roach per year for every inhabitant of the country. So much did unique Azov once produce! The 3,000 tons now caught there are mainly anchovy and goby.

In recent years the level of Azov has fallen by over two meters, despite the avowals of the planners of the celebrated Volga-Don, Tsimliansk Sea, and other water systems in this area, who promised a fall of only 40 centimeters at most. The waters of the Don and Kuban are dispersed for irrigation, and the decrease in river runoffs leads to an influx of saline waters from the Black Sea. This also has a harmful effect on the fish shoals.

The forecast *Nature 1980* concludes that the Sea of Azov will lose its value as a fishing ground by 1980. It long ago became unsuitable for resorts. Indeed, this was what a high-ranking official with the State Planning Committee had in mind when he said: "We have already lost Azov, the Aral . . . and, apparently, the Caspian."

The high salinity of the Sea of Azov still blocks the development of eutrophication in it, but in all other characteristics it is already comparable with the notorious Lake Erie. Here, at Azov, we have caught up with America. And gone ahead, since Erie was never the nation's marine larder, as was Azov.

After the seas the rivers are lost. In the basins of the Kuban, Don, and Terek rivers, irrigated agriculture is being intensively developed. But almost half of the water that does not reach the Sea of Azov disappears here senselessly:[3] it either evaporates or percolates, turning the ground into swamp.

At the same time, reclamation systems have caused the mass death of fish. They go up the channels into the rice fields, where they dry out or suffocate from lack of oxygen in the stagnant water of the very channels.

Fishermen's claims against the Kuban Irrigation Construction Trust in 1974-76 reached 30 million rubles per year. The claims against a trust building similar systems on the Don were 16 million rubles.

The Azov, the Don, and the Kuban are paying for the incompetency of the country's collective farming system. The fish, and indeed the entire biological system of the rivers and the Sea of Azov, are sacrificed for the sake of a monetary increase in the grain harvest. For the sake of wheat and rice which, if agriculture were better organized, could be obtained in other areas and by other, simpler means.

The mathematicians of Rostov-on-Don have created a complicated system of models that theoretically permit one to solve the problem of optimal use of Azov basin waters. To have, as they say, their cake and eat it too. These models received quite flattering appraisals from mathematicians and ecologists alike. However, when the question was posed of applying these models to the development of the economy in other areas, one of our leading specialists on ecological problems said:

> The Rostov models are good in themselves. But so far they have added neither fish nor rice. I don't know how the Rostov planners have been using them, but to propagandize these models now is advertising turned upside down.

The lack in reclamation systems of channels for the passage of fish to spawn is a serious problem.

Of the 250 large water-sharing systems operating in the country, only eighty-five have fish runs. Fish runs are now being added to some of them, but at almost half (103) they are not even in the drafting stage. Science, of course, can contribute appreciably to conservation in our country. But much more important here is the simple implementation of simple measures: e.g., setting up and observing rules, and so on Yet this is what proves most complicated.

V. Kunin, the late director of the Institute of Water Problems and corresponding member of the Academy of Sciences, wrote that nine out of ten complex problems with water in the USSR are administrative and organizational, not scientific.

Many of our woes undoubtedly derive from the fact that water costs practically nothing in our country. Virtually all experts dealing with water believe that the lack of cost for one of the most valuable natural resources is absurd. Even the periodical *Communist* wrote that "the lack of a price for water does not promote a prudent attitude toward it."[4] Lemeshev, the author of the article, cites glaring examples: the water consumed in smelting a ton of steel of the same grade varies from 25 to 764 tons depending on whether water is plentiful in the region around the foundry. (One French firm uses one ton of water for one ton of steel.) Despite an order from the Ministry of the Petroleum Industry, many businesses are even now pumping clean water from rivers and lakes into oil strata instead of used stratal water. And so on.

We know that a number of academicians and professors, including Lemeshev, have often tried to persuade government agencies to abandon the idea of "cost-free water." In doing so they cite the experience of socialist Czechoslovakia. But at the level of the Central Committee of the Communist Party they received an abrupt "no," since this would "contradict the principles of a socialist economy," where cost is determined only by social labor invested, and no one has invested labor in the water of the rivers and lakes.

But there is no denying the multitude of facts showing that free water is detrimental to the conservation of water resources. Cannot the ideologues recognize that the principles of socialist economics contradict the interests of preserving our environment? . . .

The pollution of our rivers and seas with sodium, chlorine, and sulfur salts is considered almost harmless, since sea water contains these salts.

However, the water from rivers in industrial regions sometimes is saltier than the water of the seas into which they flow. The Ingulets, the Northern Donets, and the Samara, which are all part of the basins of the Black and Azov seas, contain 20 to 25 parts per thousand of salts. But pure sea water is rich in living organisms and fish, while these rivers have been turned into sewers no one goes near unless absolutely necessary.

The water from mines, quarries, and ore-concentrating mills has polluted the rivers and tributaries of the Urals. The local inhabitants do not use the water from the Tanalyk River and other bodies of water in the southern Urals even to scrub their floors. This water is totally black, and the only signs of life visible are strands of dull brown, slimy algae.

Two cubic kilometers of saline water (from 3 to 25 parts per thousand) drain into the seas from the mines and quarries of the European part of the USSR alone.

Up to ten million tons of various mineral salts are discharged into the Baltic. For the shallow Sea of Azov the figure is three million. (The Rhine, which has been dubbed the sewer of Western Europe, discharges only 430,000 tons of such compounds into the North Sea.)

More than one million tons of various salts accumulate every year in the Dniepr, particularly in its reservoirs. At the same time, the shortage of fresh water in the central Ukraine worsens.

Yet the ways to reduce or even completely stop mineral pollution are striking in their simplicity and availability. Eighty percent of the Krivoi Rog shaft water could be used on site for magnetic ore concentration An experiment at the Zyrianov plant in the Altai showed that saline water is even preferable for such processes.

Promising experiments have also been carried out on the use of brackish water for irrigation. With skillful watering brines do not salinize the soil either in the south, near Zaporozhe, nor in the north, near Leningrad in the Kingisepp District. Because of lack of funds, even these experiments have not gone beyond one or two state farms, have not been translated into projects for using saline water in the combines of the Kola Peninsula.

All the prospects for developing the economy in the Ukraine

depend on the channeling of water from the Danube. A simple calculation shows that a cubic meter of Danube water costs 1.5-2.0 rubles, while a cubic meter of shaft water after desalinization costs 0.2-0.5 rubles. However, the Ministry of the Coal Industry and the Ministry of Ferrous Metallurgy are supposed to desalinate these waters, and the cost of desalinization makes each ton of coal and steel 20 to 50 kopecks more expensive. Naturally, neither ministry wants this. The funds for channeling the waters from the Danube must be taken from another government pocket—from the Ministry of Water Resources and Reclamation . . . which maintains that shaft waters are not its concern.

Modern methods using membranes have been developed for desalinization. With them each cubic meter of desalinized water costs 3 to 4 kopecks rather than 20 to 50. At the laboratory level Soviet chemists have perfected these same processes using polyamide films, and now a factory that distills 43,000 cubic meters of water per day has begun operations on this basis in Saudi Arabia.

But in the Soviet Union there are no funds even for the designing and development of similar systems, and steadily growing mineral pollution continues to destroy about 1,000 rivers and streams throughout the country.

On the other hand, mineral pollution actually does seem harmless and safe if it is compared with the effects of water pollution by heavy metals.

"Compared with the heavy metals, potassium cyanide is child's play," an ecologist-hygienist once observed. "It decomposes in a few hours; but mercury, arsenic, cadmium, lead, and beryllium are another story. . . ."

Lead pollution, like oil pollution, long ago ceased to be a privilege merely of Western countries. In 1976, at a conference in Kalinin, experts from various republics surprised one another with their figures on lead in various bodies of water. In many areas it exceeded 5 to 6 MPCs. Health experts found signs of "lead apathy"—retarded development—and even cases of lead penetrating sex cells in many children from large cities. All this had been described earlier for New York.

More and more often boron and beryllium—ingredients in rocket fuel—are turning up in the waters of our rivers. Boron is present in the mineral waters of many health resorts, although extreme concentrations of it produce an opposite effect, particularly leading to impotence in men. In 1975 the magazine *Sanitation and Hygiene* described some studies in city X (Tatarsk in

Novosibirsk Province, which, of course, was not named). The boron concentration in the drinking water there was 0.5-5 milligrams per liter. About 50 percent of the men in the susceptible age group suffered impotence. Even before total impotence sets in, boron causes various changes in the gonads, and the children of these people are born with defects.

It is difficult to exaggerate the danger of heavy metals. Even silver, which has always been considered a salubrious metal, and justly so, can seriously damage an organism in large concentrations. Doctors have prescribed water containing electrolytically dissolved silver for drinking by athletes, astronauts, and some sick people. Only after rigorous experiments on white mice was it found that silver also causes changes in the sex cells. After a month of drinking "silvered water," molecules of the metal began to "glitter" in the spermatazoa of male mice.

Scientific institutions cannot study all the new metals and their compounds that get into rivers and lakes. The determination of the maximum permissible concentration of just one substance takes about eighteen months and costs 50,000 rubles. Industry is developing much more rapidly than our medicine and hygiene.

Yet fifteen years ago Soviet hygiene was recognized as a leader the world over. We were whole decades ahead, it appeared, of all other countries.

"Excursions into history aren't needed. Let's not dilate on 1944," said one specialist in a conversation, "although during the war we had adopted probably the most rigorous standards in the world for drinking water. Remember how not very long ago, in the late sixties, we sat at international forums, so to speak, at the head of the table, were mentors, teachers. . . ."

Soviet health experts today are still as strong as before in everything concerning occupational diseases and epidemiology. But our current institutes cannot keep up with research in all areas of ecology. However, new ones are set up quite slowly and, what is no less important, are located in various agencies that perform other functions.

Discussions about a single service for environmental conservation that would have both organs of control and power have been going on for more than a year; but when finally will it be set up and how effective will it be?

Nonetheless inertia and inflexibility are not the worst property of our bureaucracy. Worse by far is the energy and vigor with which it defends its own interests. As we have noted, the determination of maximum permissible norms for pollutants is a complicated and expensive matter. Many countries have pooled their efforts in this field. Collaboration between the Soviet Union and the Americans has been quite fruitful. However, only up to the point at which the Americans proposed a broad program for setting standards (i.e., MPCs) for almost all known pollutants at the same time. This program was called the Stanford Program and provided for the gathering of a large quantity of information about pollutants, their migration in nature, and their influence on the human organism. But data on the pollution of bodies of water and territory in the USSR were dubbed "strategic information" by the Soviet side, and the Soviet Union refused to participate in the Stanford Program.

Which is quite comprehensible: collecting these data would mean exposing the somber reality concealed behind the showcase. What would the criticism of the flaws of capitalism and the lauding of the advantages of our socialist system be worth in the light of accurate figures? Hence "socialist nature" is a lady of the very highest principles—she never exposes herself to strangers. Why do the United States and other Western countries openly publish statistics on pollution without fear of giving away their secrets? Probably it is "their way" . . .

If proof is needed that the showcase is no invention, it exists. If proof is needed to show that ideological impact is more important to the ruling bureaucracy than the harm done to the health of people and nature in their own country, it is on hand.

Now that the Stanford Program, which costs $2 billion, has been carried out, the Americans no longer so openly share the results of their studies. More exactly, they do not share what this program has given them. And it has yielded a surprisingly large amount: in just two years the United States got exact or approximate standards for 17,000 pollutants and many of their compounds!

By comparison Soviet scientists in these two years set MPCs for 15 of the 300 most important pollutants!

Without American help the USSR can contemplate such success in standard-setting in about eight to ten years. How many thousands of people will become ill or lose their health completely because Soviet scientists are unable to control the contamination of water with new polymers and heavy-metal compounds?

What harm will our rivers and their denizens suffer because

setting standards for dangerous pollutants is five to ten years behind?

A vital and crucial step could have been taken for the sake of the nation's health, for the sake of nature's health. It was not taken. "Strategic interests" again proved to be more important than the interests of the well-being of people and of nature.

A famous expert once concluded a talk, "The Americans set about preserving nature with purely American seriousness. They have already caught up with us in many respects, and I will not be surprised if in ecology as well, they soon, figuratively speaking, will be walking on the moon. And we will look up at them from below and write that nonetheless we were first . . ."

# 4 Secret Land

The chapter entitled "Land Use" in the book *Hundred Year War* by the American judge William O. Douglas, begins with lines from T. S. Eliot.

What are the roots that clutch, what branches grow
Out of this stony rubbish? Son of man,
You cannot say, or guess, for you know only
A heap of broken images, where the sun beats,
And the dead tree gives no shelter, the cricket no relief,
And the dry stone no sound of water. Only
There is shadow under this red rock,
(Come in under the shadow of this red rock),
And I will show you something different from either
Your shadow at morning striding behind you
Or your shadow at evening rising to meet you;
I will show you fear in a handful of dust.

Certainly these poetic lines say no less about the fact that man's deeds are everywhere similar than the very text of Douglas's book or the fact of its translation into Russian.

The land is mankind's principal treasure and undoubtedly its most ancient. That is probably why we know so many ways to destroy it.

Like everything old and historical, these ways do not suit us and our contemporaries, and we are finding new ways to turn the land to dust and nothingness. One way is better than the others.

In contrast to other problems, wastefulness in the use of land is not a secret in the Soviet Union. Much has been said and written about the thousands of hectares of fertile soil that have been set aside for factories, mines, and power lines.

Other problems did not come up, and it seemed there was no reason for them to.

Around 1975-76, when special soil laboratories were set up, it was found that the country's fields and pasturelands were contaminated with 150 kinds of pesticides, poisonous chemicals, and trace elements.

Naturally everything industry tosses into the "dump above" in the end accumulates in the sea or in the soil. About ninety compounds of heavy metals are now found in our soil.

The experience of other countries is reason enough to treat such facts seriously. Soviet studies on the migration of these compounds in the soil have just begun, but American scientists, for example, have discovered that mercury spreads up to 200 meters from its source. It was found in ears of corn, although the field in question had never been treated with mercury compounds. It was later possible to determine that a lake was located 200 meters from the field into which sewage containing mercury strictly within the established limits was discharged. With time mercury accumulated and spread with the ground water.

An enormous amount of mercury is consumed by our chemical industry in the production of caustic soda. The standard permits 396 grams to escape for each ton of product; however, in many plants up to 500 grams escape, while at the Solikamsk combine 1,100 grams are lost. Leaky, defective equipment is the culprit. In Finnish and Japanese production only 20 to 30 grams per ton are lost, i.e., 12 to 25 times less.

The local inhabitants of Uzbekistan never pick the largest watermelon or musk melon in the market. Giant melons can now be grown simply by applying huge quantities of fertilizers, particularly saltpeter. Fortunately, saltpeter, which concentrates in the melon pulp, makes them bitter, so that cases of serious poisoning are comparatively rare.

In recent years more and more sludge and sediments from purifying equipment have been used as fertilizer. Such sludge improves the soil with large quantities of organic substances, but it also bears large quantities of trace elements that accumulate in grain and fruit.

Unfortunately, hopes of closing the disrupted cycle by converting municipal wastes into fertilizer for fields have not worked out. Composts made from refuse (by a French procedure) from one of Moscow's factories subsequently proved to be saturated with carcinogenic chemical compounds and metals. Naturally, all the vegetables nourished on these composts in suburban garden plots were pumped full of them.

Now, with our inherent modesty, we can say that somehow we have achieved a certain brilliance in poisoning ourselves. With the purest cucumber, with the freshest tomato—only from gardens and without any chemical treatment—we get our share of carcinogens.

Another source of soil and water pollution is the large livestock breeding complexes. As is known, such complexes pollute the environment more than the average factory. The American approach to the intensification of livestock breeding, itself rather ecologically suspect, has been made even worse by the helplessness of our agriculture in matters of environmental protection. The trace elements, hormone preparations, and antibiotics force fed to animals on these farms are, of course, dispensed not strictly "scientifically." And even with careful dosage, a considerable portion of these compounds ends up in manure and from there passes into the soil and ground water. And it goes on into plants and into crops.

The runoff from a trough containing 1,000 tons of silage pollutes a river as much as the sewage from a city of 16,000 inhabitants.

The liquid wastes from farms carry, among other things, antibiotics into the rivers. Today's tremendous rise in allergic diseases is linked not only to excessive drug use but also to the saturation of river water and food products with various kinds of fungi and trace elements.

It is hard to talk about reliable treatment of farm sewage when even pharmaceutical plants cannot guarantee it. A spot check of such plants in the Central Volga Region found huge quantitites of antibiotics and other chemical medicinal preparations in their sewage.

Enemy No. 1 for soil fertility was once industry. Now, however, reclamation has unquestionably assumed first place. The word's etymology suggests improvement.

The campaign to drain ten million hectares in the non-black-earth belt from the very outset appeared to be baseless propaganda. The very neatness of the figure ten million suggests exaggeration. And indeed it exceeded two to three times both the land reserves and the technical, scientific, and organizational capacities of the land reclaimers.

Nonetheless the sacramental figure did its job. Science was called on to demonstrate its rationality and, most important, the possibility of achieving it in an impossible time—ten years.

Among all my numerous acquaintances who are land reclaimers and soil scientists, I cannot think of one who did not think that fulfilling the sacrosanct plan figures would be achieved at the price of the degradation of nature, that the pursuit of inflated figures of land area would lead to the depletion of the soil.

And before the start of work in the non-black-earch belt, it was known that hasty drainage of swampland would lead to excessive drying of rivers, to the destruction of berrying and hunting grounds. But the ambitious plans dictated both the pace and quality of the work.

Even at the stage of planning the land reclamation systems and soil studies, specialists talked about the shortcomings of these work methods. The drawbacks were again rooted in timetables compressed by a factor of ten and the low level of competence of the soil scientists, who had no experience with reclamation.

The local joke—"the reclaimers have adopted the slogan 'Turn all swamps into deserts!'"—rather accurately conveyed the burden of what happened.

An article by Professor Kiselev of Minsk, published in the magazine *Nature* (1972, no. 12), is cited by many experts as a very thorough and uncompromising analysis of what was done in celebrated Polesie.

Weather station data, asserted Kiselev, had long indicated Polesie had ceased to be the water-logged region it had once been, and which from sheer inertia the newspapers and the Ministry of Water Resources and Reclamation still claimed it to be. Superficial and arbitrary views had once set drainage figures for Polese, and since then no one has revised them, despite the parlous results.

Kiselev's studies, done quite late, after millions of hectares had been drained, showed that it had been possible to drain only selectively, in small patches, and some places had not been drained at all.

The paradox of Byelorussian Polesie is its extraordinary mosaic of soils: sandy, peat, gley, etc. Often drainage had the effect that on hills sandy soils dried out but were turned into blown sand. Peat soils played "a different trick" on the reclaimers. After reclamation everything dried out on these soils, although the ground water was just below the roots. For wheat or beets to grow on this former swampland they had to be watered, and not simply watered but sprinkled. In the last ten years the swampy Polesie has learned that there are such things as dust storms.

Even a technique designed for other regions of the country proved to be unsuitable. Stubbing machines tore up the thin layer of humus along with the brush roots. Ordinary plow blades plowed sand up to the surface . . .

Thus it is now conceded even officially that despite the considerable capital investment, reclamation yields a variable increment to production. In the official lexicon "variable" means little or nothing.

Drainage added thousands of new hectares but made old farmland worthless. Then they began to quickly plant pines on the old and newly draining land. If it wasn't farmland, let it be forest! But the forest also soon withered. As Kiselev established, pines require acid soils, which are formed where water is stagnant. The drainage canals increased flow, and within five to seven years the frail saplings fell prey to insects or viral diseases. Then the ailing new plantings began to infect the old forests . . .

The main harm could have been avoided, writes Kiselev, if the former swamps had been turned into meadow rather than plow land. The well-developed livestock industry of Lithuania, Estonia, and Latvia relied on meadows and pastures of exactly this sort. But in Byelorussia the plan targets stipulated arable land, and that was that.

The soil complexes in almost all swampy areas, and not just Polesie, are paradoxical. That is why they have remained undeveloped. However, the experience in Polese has taught almost nothing to those who are planning and directing reclamation in Kalinin, Iaroslav, and other regions.

Of course, the differences between reclamation in the Baltic republics and in Polesie or in the Non-Black-Earth Region lie not merely in plan figures for arable and meadow land. The distinction here lies mainly in social and historical conditions.

In Estonia the soils are even poorer and rockier than in the Iaroslav or Kalinin regions, but in Estonia reclamation has produced excellent results because each clump of earth has been approached personally, thoughtfully. Broad land drainage was begun in Estonia in the midtwenties, and most of it was done during the period of private farms. One can imagine that the attitude of the farmer toward his own land and toward his own swamp was as different as night from day from the attitude of today's collective farm workers toward their land, which belongs to nobody. They have practically ceased to be materially dependent on the land; and after long years of help from the collective farm system, it seems they have been completely freed from subjective attachment as well.

One need only imagine for a moment how attentively the farmer followed the work of the experts, the construction of the canals, each degree of their slope. And picture also the sense of responsibility of the reclaimers to understand that the present system, in which everything from the soil banks to the digging of the canals is done by outsiders, people unknown either to each other or to the collective farm workers (and everything is done in a hurry, with no accountability to the farm workers)—this present system cannot help but destroy at least half of the "improved" land.

It is said that the private landowner thinks only about his own field. But the fact is that the bourgeois, private property period conserved more public lands—hunting grounds, berry fields, etc.—than all now being preserved by reclamation in any region. And that is today, after public ownership of natural benefits has become an established fact.

The very system of land "improvement" is harmful where the sole client of any reclamation is not those who work the land and who, on paper, own it but the Ministry of Agriculture and its countless departments in each region and district. The job of the officials is to fulfill plan targets, and the problems of the individual farm do not concern them. Each year on the collective farms to the north of the Iaroslav region, as much pasture and plow land becomes overgrown because there is no one to work it as is added by reclamation. Within a few years even reclaimed land will begin to grow over . . . but the plan will have been fulfilled!

The beautiful Crab Lakes lie between Leningrad and Vyborg. At one time, when not only crabs but wildlife as well abounded there, they were called the Swan Lakes and were known in the hunting world throughout Europe. Something of their former glory has survived to our day. However, a nearby state farm had a reclamation plan, and it had to be fulfilled. Some of the lakes were emptied. Of course, this caused great harm to both the fishing industry and to migratory birds. But in this case it is important that the draining of the silty shallows added not a single hectare of new meadowland to the state farm.

It was known beforehand that this would be the case, and the farm probably didn't even need the land. In what other economy would it be possible to squander thousands of rubles digging drainage canals and destroying lakes when it was known beforehand that no one would benefit at all from it? . . .

To start this chapter we quoted lines by an American poet. The story of the Crab Lakes recalls the lines of a Russian writer. In the middle of the nineteenth century, Aleksei Konstantinovich Tolstoy foresaw some of the features of twentieth-century Soviet Russia with striking accuracy in his "Ballad with a Bias." Here are some of the truly immortal lines in that poem:

> Here you have a real paradise!
> Really everything is splendid!
> But this flourishing garden
> Will soon be planted with turnips!
> "What a misfortune!"
> Exclaimed the bride,
> "Has the vegetable patch really
> No room for turnips?"
> And he answered: "Lada, my dear!
> There is certainly a spot for turnips,
> But we have to ruin the garden
> Because it is for flowers!"
>
> . . .
>
> They want to flatten the whole world
> And thus introduce equality,
> They want to spoil everything
> For the common good.

writes A. K. Tolstoy about the pioneers in exploiting natural beauty. He dedicates his ballad to the "Russian commune"— "Russian commune, take my first experience"—and judging from the story of the Crab Lakes, and from many other instances, the message was right on target.

The creation of new farmland in Central Asia is becoming more and more questionable and expensive. According to data of Uzbek scientists, water lost through evaporation and filtration in the Karakum and Southern Fergan canals is 40 and even 70 percent of the total water volume.[1]

To dig one kilometer of the Karakum Canal bulldozers had to destroy up to 50 hectares of land suitable for irrigation in the surrounding area. For dozens of kilometers on either side of the canal, all the wells and springs are drying up. According to other statistics, from 40 to 50 percent of all irrigation water is wasted. The wise rules governing distribution of water and irrigation, which formerly had been as sacred to the local inhabitants as the laws of the Koran, are either difficult to enforce over the vast expanses of modern fields or are simply disregarded. As a result, today in Uzbekistan approximately every fifth hectare of the 3.7 million hectares of irrigated land suffers irrigation erosion, and 90 percent of all the land has undergone some kind of erosion! About 1.5 million hectares of land in Uzbekistan have had to be abandoned in recent years (since the end of the fifties) because of salinization and erosion. In Turkmenia 10,000 hectares of land were abandoned each year during the midsixties, and now this figure has grown to 15,000. The gray desert soils that predominate in these republics are easily washed away by clumsy waterings, and in one season up to a hundred tons of soil are stripped from one hectare of an irrigated cotton field.

Often the irrigation system as a whole causes irreversible changes in the ecology of barren lands. The Ashkhabad Institute for Desert Lands has developed a few simple methods for water management, based on popular experience. But evidently such devices as digging holes in the takyr desert soil and storing the spring rains in them for an entire summer seem too primitive for twentieth-century Soviet Central Asia. In any case, these promising methods for protecting the earth from salinization and depletion have so far found no application.

In steppe and semisteppe Kalmykia, all the present wasteland was formed solely where reclamation and plowing had been done. But to this very day the Kalmyk steppes are tilled...

The senseless plowing of the Kazakh steppes has in fifteen years generated three million hectares of sand...

All the major rivers in Central Asia have been almost completely wrecked for irrigation. Yet at the same time, at the Chardzhou Hydroelectric Power Plant on the Syr-Daria River, during the floods every year millions of cubic meters of water pour pointlessly into the Arpasai Basin, which has no outlet. The designers from the Hydrological Planning Institute had at some point cut costs on the flood drains...

In Central Asia land conservation is more closely linked to water conservation than ever before. In Uzbekistan today there are about 25,000 active artesian wells, and almost 20 percent of them pour out their water without any use, forming lakes and ponds around them. There are no valves or taps on them, so 100 million cubic meters of water are lost every year. Such fountains in the Besharyk District have considerably increased the salinity of the soil and ground water.

In Turkmenia unsystematic cattle-grazing on the slopes of Koped-Dag and Kugin-Tag has sharply reduced the growth area of wild pomegranate, pistachio, and fig, which play a major role in preventing mountain slopes from becoming wasteland. These plants are just as important in the ecology of local fauna: they provide food for large animals—the wild boar, the wild goat, the gazelle, and the wolf—as well as for birds—the rock partridge and the black vulture. In addition they provide shelter and nesting places for birds.

Breeders note another priceless property of wild plants: the genetic stock of these strikingly hardy and unassuming trees is necessary for the development of new varieties of fruit, although grazing and the uprooting of the wild thickets are threatening to destroy them too.

For a long time an Ashkhabad glass factory used as packing material cheap selin grass, which was mowed near the city. After a few years it was found that selin holds down sandy soil, and now without it the sands are encroaching on the city outskirts.

In Turkmenia sand, of course, surprises no one. But visitors are really amazed to see the sand creeping into the outskirts and streets of Poronaisk, a city in northern Sakhalin in the midst of formerly impassable taiga! Having cut down all their forests, the local inhabitants are now drawing on the experience of the Turkmen in their struggle with the sand dunes.

> The rich fields of corn—such was the praise for the Tula black-earth soils around Severodonetsk and Kimovsk when the coal miners arrived. Now pits, quarries, and heaps of rock rising fifty meters and more are seen everywhere. Even if seeds of grass should fall on them, it is difficult for them to sprout in soils with too much iron sulfide, which when oxidized gives off sulfuric acid. The unpleasant smell of hydrogen sulfide wafts from the dumps. . . . The water in the depths of the quarries is unfit for drinking . . . there is no life in it. . . .
>
> An equally if not more cheerless picture can be seen at mineral mining sites in the southern Urals, where some pits reach a depth of 500 meters. From the air they are like lunar craters. . . .
>
> Peat cutting causes severe damage to the natural landscape. Thermoelectric power plants strew the land with ash dumps. . . . Industrial wastes from many enterprises form vast heaps. . . .[2]

The seriousness of problems of land recultivation is acknowledged by everyone. Indeed, it is difficult to hide from people's view the ugly outskirts of dozens of cities in the Urals, the Kuznets Basin, the Don Basin, the Kola Peninsula, greater Moscow, Ekibastuz, Karaganda, and the new Achinsk Basin. They can't be screened by newspaper articles. Only the figures for land devastation for the country as a whole can be concealed. Adding together the various official statistics, one can show that the mining industry and peat production have ruined no less than 1.5-1.8 million hectares.

Experts on recultivation long ago established the following relationship: a one-hectare pit "ensures" cluttering up six hectares around it and leads to a reduction in ground water, the withering of vegetation, and other ecological depredations over a minimum of fifteen hectares and a maximum of twenty to twenty-five hectares. Considering this, one can say that pits, mines, and peat fields have devoured no less than twenty million hectares of the total land area of our country. Using the favorite newspaper analogies, this equals the area of Belgium or other small countries: seven little Belgiums or one considerable West Germany.

Each year another 100,000 hectares are added to these lands.

Each year some land is recultivated, restoring its more or less natural appearance. The press and the cinema eagerly report such facts.

Five hundred hectares of forest are growing on the dumps near Tula . . . On nearby dumps oats have been sown . . . In Georgia former manganese mines support good vineyards . . . The land is being restored in the shale areas of Estonia and in the southern Ukraine . . . The successful recultivation of the waste heaps near Karaganda provoked considerable interest at the international exposition in Spokane . . .

There is plenty of information. However, if someone needs the overall figures for the achievements of recultivation for the country, he will not find them in any article or handbook.

Each ministry, each administrative board zealously reports its achievements or plans for achievements but wants to know nothing about the problem in general, about how it looks on a national scale.

Summarizing data from various articles, the total land area "put in order" each year must amount to 8,000-12,000 hectares. In other words, 8 to 12 percent of what is destroyed by mines, quarries, and open pits every year. Millions of hectares of old mine pits and dumps remain in their former frightful state, and only a small portion of them are beginning to grow over naturally. Millions of hectares are devoured by other branches of industry as well.

M. N. Miliutin, a deputy minister of the chemical industry, proudly writes that soon "the nation's chemicals industry" will recultivate 900 hectares each year.[3] What part of this is the ground "the nation's chemicals industry" destroys during the same year, if just a few potassium plants appropriate 500 to 600 hectares for dumping their wastes?[4]

Tailings and slag heaps, ash piles and city dumps cover about five million hectares across the country (1.7 Belgiums). Each year more land is appropriated for them than for pits and mines: 200,000 to 300,000 hectares. Furthermore, whereas before only abandoned land was used for them, now more often dumps are biting into agricultural land.

Until 1990, and possibly even longer, a large portion of municipal refuse will not be processed in special plants but will be carried away to dumps, as was done a hundred and a thousand years ago.

Some new areas for burying garbage, so-called polygons, actually do effectively isolate industrial and municipal wastes. Such an area was built near Leningrad, for example. But examples of such polygons throughout the country remain few, and all the old huge dumps seriously pollute the air, the soil, and the ground water.

In Kursk the dump outside the city burns not only harmless paper but also the wastes from a rubber factory and a battery factory. Next to the incinerator site is one of the last parcels of natural steppe——the Strelets Steppe, part of the Kursk Preserve. As early as 1973 experts from the Institute of Geography of the USSR Academy of Sciences confirmed that the accumulation of toxic compounds drifting from the huge round-the-clock fires was causing irreversible changes in plants and in the composition of the soils in the preserve.[5] The smoke has even begun to harm the famous Kursk nightingales, whose nesting area is still located in the groves not far from the Strelets Steppe. Krasnitskii, director of the preserve, has more than once appealed to common sense, to social conscience, both in print and at various conferences. In 1973, after geographers, led by Academician Gerasimov, spoke out, the dump was almost closed; but then the fires flared anew, and they burn to this day.

In addition to the ways I have described, which are the

same the world over, to reduce the area of fertile and life-sustaining land, there is one other. Its embodiment and further development, if not its invention, are undoubtedly achievements of the USSR.

I mean the flooding of land with the waters of major reservoirs. Unlike the United States, Canada, and other countries, the USSR has built huge hydroelectric power plants on floodplain rivers where reservoirs spread out horizontally and lay waste to priceless marsh lands. Twelve million hectares (120,000 square kilometers)—four Belgiums!—have been turned by us into the bottoms of such reservoirs.

The Dniepr Hydroelectric Power Plant was, of course, the first such colossus. A few years ago, colleagues of the eminent hydrologist Professor Vendrov calculated that merely the hay harvested from the areas flooded by the Dniepr plant, if used as fuel, would yield as much energy as is put out by the power plant.

Huge hydroelectric power plants solve one energy problem while creating dozens of others. The money spent to control erosion of the shores of the Dniepr reservoirs and to combat the seemingly indestructible blue-green algae has long since exceeded the short-term advantages the power plant once yielded.

The huge Kuibyshev Sea on the Volga inundated 20,000 square kilometers, and 11,700 of them have now become problem "shallows." Simply put, they are now silted, impassable swamps, where masses of algae multiply in the summer and then rot . . .

The Rybinsk Sea, once the largest artificial body of water in the world, flooded the best meadows and lands in northern Iaroslav Province, inundating oak groves and other valuable forests. Four hundred and ninety-seven villages and seven cities had to be relocated outside the inundated area. In operation fewer than twenty years, the Rybinsk Hydroelectric Power Plant for some reason has proved behind "the state of the art" of modern energy systems, and its future is very much in doubt. If the forests and the lands now at the bottom of the sea could be restored to agricultural use, the Rybinsk Sea would be drained in the next couple of years.

The methods of hydraulic engineering have changed little over the years. Even now, at the end of the seventies, the magazine *Science and Life* (1977, no. 3) writes proudly about the Zeisk Hydroelectric Power Plant, now under construction, that no forests will be cut in the basin of the future plant . . . According to the clever plan of the engineers, "when it is filled, the spring ice will tear the forest from the bottom." What then happens to the trees is clear. Some will again sink and rot in the water, while others will be tossed onto the shore and rot there.

Even with the chronic shortage of paper and cellulose in the country, there has been no case in hydraulic engineering practice in which the forests in the flood zone were completely removed. It never occurred to anyone to strip and remove priceless Ukrainian black-earth or other soils, although it is difficult to overestimate the ecological and economic value of these soils. With them it would have been possible to repair the wounds inflicted on the land in all sectors of industrial activity as well as to improve eroded land. Finally, resting on the bottom of the reservoirs, the rich soils serve as the source of nutrients for excessive growth of algae (eutrophication).

The S. Ia. Zhuk Chief Institute of the Hydrological Planning Agency has plans to construct huge hydroelectric power plants downstream on the Ob, Lena, Enisei, and Indigirka rivers. The reservoirs formed by these plants would cover 300,000 square kilometers and cause extensive climatic changes.

More than likely, these ecologically absurd plans will remain unrealized, but dozens of other power plants, built on river flood plains, will in the next few years inundate another 13 million hectares (130,000 square kilometers).

Above a dam the reservoirs inundate the land, while below it the meadows and deltas often dry up. This was what happened with the Ili River after the Kapchagai Power Plant was built, despite protests from the Kazakh Academy of Sciences and an extensive discussion in the press.[6] The Kapchagai Sea near Alma-Ata doomed the lower Ili and half of Lake Balkhash to drying up.

The designers of the Kapchagai Power Plant, the experts of the Hydrological Planning Agency, would have it no other way, pointing to the 700,000 hectares of new land that would be restored to life by irrigation. It turned out later that these figures were at least 100 times too high! But that was later; while at the crucial moment the Hydrological Planning Agency defended its offspring and the Kapchagai plant was constructed exactly as it had originally been designed. Some gross errors were rectified after the plant was already in operation.

On a few occasions even the official press revealed that the arguments of the Hydrological Planning Agency were either outright deception of the public or illiterate voluntarism with regard to nature. This voluntarism translated into an unequivocal loss to both the ecology and the economy of the country; nonetheless the agency flourishes as before. This organization, now called an institute, has a good dozen branch institutes throughout the country. In Moscow the parent institute, near the Sokol subway stop, has a modern skyscraper familiar to Muscovite and visitor alike. The Leningrad branch occupies a whole block on the Petrograd side, and huge institutes are operating in Kharkov, Kuibyshev, and Tashkent under the aegis of the same agency. This organization has now been assigned the construction of hydroelectric power plants in foreign countries and the main development of water-supply systems for atomic power plants.

What is the basis for its unshakable authority? Why is it always right, despite all the facts exposing it?

What newspaper and magazine articles pass over in silence is chronicled in the files of the professional journal *Hydrochemical Construction*, particularly in their obituaries for the late directors of the Hydrological Planning Agency, Academician S. Ia. Zhuk, Ia. D. Rappoport, and others. They tell the story of an organization that began with the White Sea-Baltic Canal. One of the sections of the State Political Administration (GPU—secret police) in charge of construction gave birth to the Hydrological Planning Agency.

Until the 1950s all hydraulic engineering in the USSR was done by one of the daughter enterprises of the GPU. Officially it was called the Main Hydrological Construction Agency of the NKVD (MVD, MGB). The managers of the Hydrological Planning Agency had the rank of major generals: Zhuk, Rappoport, and Zhurin. Some of the projects they completed were: the White Sea Canal, the Moscow-Volga Canal, the Rybinsk Hydroelectric Power Plant, the Volga-Don, and others.

There is far more important information about the history of hydroelectric construction in the USSR in Alexander Solzhenitsyn's *Gulag Archipelago* than in all the textbooks on hydraulic engineering. The *Archipelago* gives some idea of the attitude toward nature in the '30s and '40s. Even the most brilliant articles on ecology will remain superficial without an accurate history of our society over the last few decades.

For instance, where are the carp and roach that disappeared from the Azov, and where is the notorious GPU? Where is the shortage of fodder on the collective farms in Central Russia, and where are the repressions of the '30s and '40s? In the chain of causes between them there is one link—the Hydrological Planning Agency, with its voluntaristic attitude toward nature. Ecological connections inevitably entail historical ones.

The fact that the development of energy production in the USSR took place in the most primitive, linear, and ruinous way was due not to geographical factors, not to the economics of the first five-year plans, but to the political situation at the time.

All the grandiose plans to "harness nature," to divert river courses, to correct "millenial errors by nature" were advantageous for the ruling bureaucracy purely politically, and they became facts. The economic benefits were secondary, and ecology was not taken into account at all. On the contrary, the more such projects contradicted the laws of nature, the more highly they were regarded. The more brilliantly the illusion of their success demonstrated the power and wisdom of the new leaders of the country.

The names of the managers of the building projects, the executives of the Hydrological Planning Agency, were set by prisoners into the slopes of the White Sea-Baltic Canal after the names of the leaders: Stalin—Kaganovich—Molotov—Yagoda —Firin—Rappoport—Zhuk.

And when the propaganda effect of "Stalin's grandiose plans" had been exhausted, their practical results were of little interest to the authorities. As Solzhenitsyn showed, the White Sea-Baltic Canal was negligible for the nation's economy; and for a long time now, people have known about the existence of the White Sea Canal mainly from the picture on the cigarette packet once named for it. Stalin's renowned plan to "transform nature" was only 20 percent fulfilled in its main ambition— the planting of forest belts in the south—and no more money was allocated to it. True, as far as the destruction of "old nature" is concerned, all the plans were always fulfilled and overfulfilled.

> Let the fragile green breast of Siberia be dressed in the cement armor
> of cities, armed with the stone muzzles of factory chimneys, and
> girded with iron belts of railroads. Let the taiga be burned and felled,
> let the steppes be trampled. Let this be, and so it will be inevitably.
> Only in cement and iron can the fraternal union of all peoples, the
> iron brotherhood of all mankind be forged.[7]

Prophesies, of course, tell us more about the times when they were uttered, about the times that bore them. Zazubrin blurted out this paean to the iron and cement brotherhood of all peoples in 1926, and with striking depth it communicates the mood of his times, a spirit of demolishing all nature's foundations, and, of course, not only in Siberia.

As Maxim Gorky said, the Soviet people were to make "mad rivers sane" and at the same time recast themselves in this, for the most part forced, labor.[8]

The life of society was shaped by people who knew only one truth—rout the adversary. Even if this adversary was rivers, forests, or the inimitable uniqueness of nature.

More than twenty years have passed since Stalin's death. Has much changed in our attitudes toward nature? A great deal and very little. To be sure, the Hydrological Planning Agency has long been part of the Ministry of Energy, and a department for environmental conservation has been set up within it. Also, hydroelectric power plants and canals are now built for the most part by free engineers and workers. However, the force of inertia is great: even now the efforts of the agency, more frequently than the projects of other planning institutions, do not meet the elementary requirements of ecology. Very often they turn out cheaper and simpler than other options because of "eased" measures for protecting the environment. And note one other detail: the director of the civil institute of the agency is still called the Commander of the Institute, as is done only in military services. Even now its projects, like the projects of other institutes "transforming nature," are prepared in secret from the public.

Of course, today the Hydrological Planning Agency is no longer the only institution to whose voice the State Planning Committee listens. But its voice is, in fact, the loudest, and its present influence and its history are instructive.

As long as we do not understand where the roots of our violence to nature lie, as long as we do not realize that the current secretiveness with regard to ecological statistics and ecological projects continues to feed this violence, we will never find ways to conserve our remaining valuable land and priceless, picturesque wilds.

# 5 The Law: Theory and Reality

*"The absurd severity of Russian laws is diminished by half by their chaotic enforcement."*
George Kennan, American traveler, end of the nineteenth century

On July 14, 1920, a tree was cut down on the Gorky government estate forty kilometers from Moscow. On the orders of E. Ia. Vever, director of the worker's rest home that had recently opened there, a large spruce was felled. On the very same day, July 14, A. Belenkii, the commander of Lenin's personal guard (Lenin's summer home was in the same park), drew up a protocol about the illegal felling. Lenin read the protocol and promptly ordered Vever arrested and sentenced to Podolsk Prison for one month. Lenin also ordered this sentence broken down into segments of seven to ten days, so that "neither the farmwork nor the management of the rest home would suffer the slightest harm" from the director's incarceration.

Copies of the documents concerning the Vever affair were published in Lenin's *Collected Works* (vol. 51, p. 151). The story of the illegal felling of trees became quite famous and a textbook example of the concern of the socialist government and of Lenin personally for the preservation of nature. It has been cited in the works of biologists, journalists, and ideologues. Even experts in Soviet and international law describe it as a source when they discuss the roots of our laws in the field of environmental protection.

We do not know what jurists think about the "Vever precedent" in the privacy of their homes, but there was a physicist who drew attention to the illegality of this arrest . . .

Indeed, the Constitution of the RSFSR had been formally

in effect since July 10, 1918, and it guaranteed all citizens the protection of the law in everything pertaining to the deprivation of liberty, particularly imprisonment only upon a court sentence after investigation, open trial, and so on.

Lenin, at that time chairman of the Council of People's Commissars, who had no relationship to the judicial authorities of the republic, nevertheless convicted Vever on his own initiative and, moreover, in absentia. It is clear from the documents in Volume 51 of Lenin's *Collected Works* that Vever composed his exculpatory memorandum only after his arrest, which means after sentence had been pronounced (vol. 51, p. 221).

This is the purely juridical side of the affair, but perhaps for 1920, the year of the Civil War, other factors should be considered. Let's see what they might be . . .

Was there anything especially important about this matter, i.e., Vever's crime? After all, it was only a tree . . .

Inexperience, unstable principles of power? But if Lenin, a lawyer by education who in 1918 had been chairman of the Constitutional Commission that had drawn up the Constitution, did not know the laws or procedures for the exercise of power, what can be said about the other representatives of power? . . .

Finally, what about the swiftness, the urgency of steps in the Vever affair? Vever was not at the Civil War front when he broke the law, nor was it a period of counterrevolutionary rebellion, but in the peace and quiet of the countryside. Still justice in his case came out where it had in the majority of Cheka operations.[1]

Since 1920, for more than fifty years, Soviet ideologues and law-makers have held up the Vever story as a model of Soviet legality. And to some extent one must doubtlessly agree with them. There can be no denying that in Vever's arrest, his sentence, and his imprisonment in coordination with his work at his job may be found, as in a nutshell, all the typical features of our system of justice. They reflect its fundamental property: power and the law are in the same hands.

In 1957 Estonia was the first of the union republics to adopt the Law on the Preservation of Nature. By 1963 similar laws had been passed in the other republics.

But to this day there is no analogous national law, and even theoretically it could not appear for at least a decade. There is no mention of such a law being in preparation in the plans of the Commission of the Supreme Soviet of the USSR on draft legislation; in other words, there are no plans for the introduction of proposals for such a law by the deputies of the Supreme Soviet.

Laws concerning nature in all fifteen republics, on the one hand, take care of the juridical side of nature conservation over the entire territory of the USSR, and one more national law would serve no purpose. But on the other hand, there would be no need for such a law only if all the union republics actually were sovereign and equal governments, as it appears on paper.

In practice, however, it happens that the largest industrial enterprises—and *they* are the polluters of the environment more than anyone—are accountable only to the central government. Such a factory is subject only to Moscow, and the laws of the republic where it is located are not binding on it.

The Estonian shale industry is subordinate to a Moscow administrative board, and hence the local authorities cannot demand that the mines treat the water and air, as is required by Estonian laws on environmental protection. They can only observe the carrying out of those environmental measures for which the mines get funds from the authorities in Moscow. As a result the rivers in the shale basin are the most polluted in all Estonia, and according to the forecast *Nature 1990*, by then the situation will probably have become worse.

Two hundred kilometers from the shale mines, near the Tallin resort area, the Maardu chemical combine pours out its smoke. It is the greatest air polluter along the littoral. But it too is accountable only to a Moscow administrative board, and the arms of the Estonians are too short to "pressure" this "skunk" right outside Tallin.

Hundreds of large plants in the heavy, chemical, mining, and power industries (to say nothing of defense) are in the same administrative situation. As a rule the laws of the union republics are disregarded even in the planning stage. As is known, the most important plants are designed in Moscow and Leningrad, and compliance with local legislation does not come within the duties of the planners.

The same is true for hydroelectric power plant construction, reclamation systems, and urbanization.

For the new atomic power plant on the South Bug, the Moscow Hydrological Planning Agency designed a water-cooling system in which used water would be fed back into the reservoir at a temperature of about 35°C. The Law on the Preservation of Nature of the Ukrainian SSR plainly states that the construction of open (sewage) water supply systems is prohibited if it is scientifically and technologically feasible to construct a closed recirculating system. There is no doubt that such a possibility existed at the South Bug atomic power plant, and, supported by the law, some experts insisted that a closed system be built. They said that the new reservoir would flood a great deal of valuable land, that it would aggravate the water shortage in this region, and that it would cause serious thermal pollution of the atmosphere. The designers replied that the Ukrainian law was no law for them and that the closed recirculating system would cost 1.5 million rubles more and prolong the design stage by one more year.

The conflict was taken to the Board of the Ministry of Power of the USSR, after which it got to the State Planning Committee; as usually happens, narrow industrial interests carried the day. The "cheap and quick" Hydrological Agency version was ratified.

A committee on nature conservation was created in the Ukraine ten years ago, and its chairman, V. Voltovskii, stated in an interview that the committee would check "the ecology" of absolutely all projects whose implementation could threaten nature in any way.[2] It is difficult to assess the committee's effectiveness (for example, in 1976 it vetoed 2.5 percent of 6,000 projects, and in 6 percent of the cases required modifications), but it is interesting that so large a project as the South Bug atomic power plant was not even looked into in Kiev. Everything was decided in Moscow.

The same thing happened with the project for the giant thermoelectric plant in Chigirin.

According to long-established rules of sanitation, the prescribed thirty-kilometer zone was set aside for it. However, this giant power plant, which will burn more than ten tons of coal per minute, will destroy the forests and fields over a much wider radius. Its smokestacks will emit more than one million tons of sulfur anhydride per year (about 1.5 percent of the total industrial pollution of the atmosphere for the entire country!), and its smoke will darken the blue sky at those very places in the eastern Ukraine whose beauty was celebrated by Gogol, Pushkin, and many Ukrainian poets. It will blacken with soot Chigirin itself, the birthplace of Bogdan Khmelnytsky, and the Kamenka estate, where Pushkin and many of the Decembrists stayed.

Have not the inhabitants of the Ukraine sacrificed too

much already for the sake of additional energy? The question is rhetorical, since no one has asked them about it, and they will learn of their sacrifices only post factum.

In the United States some states categorically refuse to have other, richer ones, pursuing their own private interests, locate their "dirty" industries in them. They call this a form of colonialism. When the Americans or Japanese export their "dirty" industries to the countries of Asia or Africa, the newspapers of various countries call this—justifiably—neocolonialism. The relationships between Moscow and the Estonian and Ukrainian authorities could also be called a typical example of the relationships between a metropolis and its colonies.[3] The same could be said about locating the Baikal combine not near Leningrad, in the center of the country, but in remote, poorly developed Buryatia. The difference, however, lies in the fact that in the "Russian-style colonization" the metropolis itself— Russia and its inhabitants—gains nothing, while Russian nature is exploited and destroyed hardly less than nature in the other fourteen republics.

Even as the republic laws on nature conservation were being passed, jurists made some rather harsh critical comments. About the Ukrainian law of 1960 it was written: "It contains no sanctions and does not spell out responsibility for breaking the law. It is powerless from its inception."[4] Another jurist summed up the weaknesses in all the republic laws on nature conservation: "All these laws are declarative and do not cover the full variety of complex relationships in the many spheres of nature conservation. They define neither the content of offenses nor the measures of liability."[5]

Time has proven the critics right. Now, after the fifteen years these laws have been in effect, one well-known jurist had the following to say about them:

> The practical implementation of the laws on nature conservation and, above all, the application of punitive measures are characterized by the following. First, punitive measures are not applied to the fullest. Second, they are applied unjustly. Third, in the vast majority of cases they are not applied at all. Too often these measures—a fine or rarely a suspended prison sentence—are not commensurate with the magnitude of the harm done to nature; they are much lighter. Too often a punitive measure lacks any moral force, since it is not the real culprit who sits in the dock but someone who has carried out illegal orders. Both the judge and the defendant know this, and the trial is turned into a game. Everyone knows that a factory's

attitude toward the environment depends heavily on instructions from the industrial section of the local party district or municipal committee, on their need to produce a plan at any price. However, a district committee gives its instructions in such a way that there is no law under which it can be construed to be accountable.

Furthermore, there is the economic justification of a punishment. Suppressive measures should influence how an enterprise or an industrial sector in general subsequently behaves. But I know of no measure that would reduce the economic incentive for an enterprise to continue breaking the law.

We are calling factories to account more often, but infractions are not becoming fewer for all that. On the contrary, their number is growing.

By no means all jurists know about the existence of some laws, to say nothing of enterprises and local authorities. In 1959 a very timely law was passed concerning a conservation area at the northern edge of some woods in the forest tundra. In the thin forest, in a zone 30 to 150 kilometers wide, all timbering was prohibited. Eleven years later, in 1970, at a conference in Sverdlovsk experts on the north said that none of the local authorities in any of the northern regions had heard a thing about such a law. Felling had gone on everywhere and is still doing so; and, of course, this helps the tundra spread south.

More and more cases concerning infractions of nature conservation laws are dealt with by arbitration within the regional executive committees and councils of ministers of the union republics rather than by the courts.

Among the graver offenses, law suits having to do with poisoning of fish in the rivers by oil spills have already become commonplace. The development of the petroleum industry has had a ruinous effect on land animals and plants as well. The fire in the oil field near Ukhta destroyed thousands of hectares of deer pasturage. Lichen, the staple of these pasture lands, grows very slowly and takes fifteen years to be restored. Such instances are occuring in the north more and more frequently.

The arbitration statistics show that laws are constantly being broken in earmarking land for large construction sites. Knowing that later it will not be so simple to get new land, every plant manager will try to get that one bit more. Even if the enterprise will actually need the land only in five to ten years, nonetheless, until then it could be plowland or meadow and yield produce. In those cases, on the other hand, when management cannot prove its claims and the land is returned to the State Land Reserve, the builders usually cut down the forests and ruin the soil with their bulldozers while litigation is pending. And none of them can be held to account for this. The government gets so many square meters back, but in what condition —this the law does not specify . . .

Reclamation systems, of course, cause great damage. In the Agrakhansk system on the Terek River, practically all the fish died, including the fry, as a result of stagnation and insufficient oxygen. The damage was estimated at 32 million rubles; but under pressure from the Council of Ministers, the arbitration board demanded only that the commercial value of the fish be repaid, leaving the loss of their offspring out of account.

A hydrolysis plant that had destroyed all the fish in the Biriusa River in the Krasnoiarsk Region had to pay several millions. This case was followed by a satirical article in *Pravda*. Shatunovskii, its author, wrote caustically about the crime of a factory manager, a person with the unlikely name of Pakintsokh, and about the negligence of the local water inspectorate. He failed to recall that twelve years before, on February 28, 1965, at the time of the campaign to save Baikal, the same *Pravda* wrote about the Biriusa plant, saying that it was polluting the river and demanding that measures be taken. But twelve years later no measures had been taken.

But finally a decision was made by the arbitration board. The day of reckoning had come for the factory; but if you think that the millions of rubles fine paid for the Biriusa River would be used to replenish the fish in the depleted stream, your thinking has nothing in common with the thinking of the government. The money was paid into the state budget, i.e., to the Ministry of Finance. This reshuffling of money from one pocket into another perhaps makes full sense to the government, but in essence it is nature that always pays.

The system of bureaucratic control is largely responsible for the poor implementation of existing laws. Even official publications cannot hush this up. O. S. Kolbasov, doctor of juridical sciences, writes in his book: "The administration and control of nature conservation embody the power of the state as regards the producer of goods and hence should actually be independent of the system they control. . . ."[6] In practice, however, they are subordinate to these departments: the Ministry of Forestry and the Timber Industry, the Ministry of Agriculture, the Ministry of Water Resources and Reclamation.

Aside from the fact that the forest, water, and soil conservation inspectorates are too dependent on the interests of their corresponding sectors of production and on their fulfillment of plans, they often lack the competence to control environmental pollution. For example, the soil conservation inspectorate has neither specialists nor instruments to measure water pollution, although in nature these things are inseparable, since practically all water pollution causes pollution of the soil and vice versa.

For their part, the departmental inspectorates complain about the contradictoriness and inadequacy of legal measures. For example, in wildlife preserves, where all hunting of animals and birds is prohibited, no punishment is provided for catching fish in the rivers on the preserves. Of course, a fish poacher can if one wishes be called to account, but on the basis of another, milder article: "unauthorized trespassing on the territory of the preserve."

The director of the Lazovskii Wildlife Preserve, which is in the Far East, once pointed out to the experts that the fine for poaching on the preserve was only ten rubles. The fine on a game reserve for the same thing, however, was much higher. Thus it cost less to poach on the most valuable natural lands.

In the domain of forest conservation, the powerlessness of the official inspectorates, coupled with the inherent flaws in Soviet legislation and existing economic structures, creates a terrible picture. Similarly, nothing can stop the senseless and merciless diminution of the Siberian forests.

Here is what an expert on forest legislation said about it:

> I try to keep a cold heart in law suits on the destruction of forests. You can't get involved in them. Five years ago I was at the giant forest station near Krasnoiarsk. I saw a whole city on the river bank. Huge cedars several arm lengths in circumference, larches, and firs lay in piles without end. And all this just lay there because the railroad had not provided freight cars. But that wasn't all. The railroad had not provided enough cars for one, two, even three years, and the forestry trust had known beforehand that there would be too few cars. Nevertheless each year more and more trees were felled. The trust had its plan. Dozens of acres of wonderful cedar taiga were uprooted, with a semidesert left in their wake—and for this the state received rotten wood. Not even timber!
>
> You may not believe me, but in my legal practice I got to see a lot of things. I got to see both murderers and victims and had to investigate crimes that defied logic. But while at the station I just got sick of it. I returned to Krasnoiarsk ill. For two days I did not leave the

hotel. The horrible thing was not the absurdity of the madness but its rationality. And of course the collective, social nature of it.

Later, on another case I got to know one of the deputies of the Supreme Soviet of the USSR; and after we had become friends, I asked him about the forest station. Why were such things going on?

"What? You don't understand? There are people out there in the taiga and they have to be paid their wages. We set up the lumber camp and brought people there. They have the right to work, and they are not responsible for our problems with the railroad cars. Don't you see? But why bother talking about it. . . ."

He told me what I already knew. For our forests there was no hope. I know that people are planting new forests and breathing life into them, but our forest area continued to shrink.

Undoubtedly all the heads of the taiga lumber enterprises knew what was happening with the half of their forest at the camp near Krasnoiarsk. And many workers surely knew. Was it necessary to confuse and corrupt people, to pervert the very notion of work, so that they would believe that turning the majestic cedar woods into mold and rot was a decent job? Was it necessary to intimidate them so that they did not dare doubt that the slogan "no unemployment under socialism" justified everything —the tremendous losses, the demise of a beauty not made by man?

Some agency set up at the government level could impartially and intelligently defend the laws on nature conservation.

The existing Interdepartmental Council, the Department on the Uses of Nature attached to the Committee on Science and Technology, and the Department on Nature Conservation of the State Planning Committee of the USSR have practically no power; furthermore, as parts of these larger bodies, they are obliged to conform to their main objectives, which are not at all oriented toward preservation of nature.

The entire system of planning and managing the economy is built on narrow industrial alignments established long ago (ferrous and nonferrous metallurgy, chemicals, petroleum processing, petroleum extraction, a multitude of branches in machine building, etc.). By their very nature ecological problems cut across many branches at once, and their resolution usually cannot help but alter the existing mode of operation of any of these branches. In other words, these problems must be solved higher up, in the USSR Council of Ministers.

As things stand now, however, the departments concerned with nature conservation can take such problems to sessions of the Council of Ministers only after approval by all the parties involved.

The Comprehensive Program for the Protection of Baikal, worked out by a commission of the Academy of Sciences in 1976, threatens to burden the Ministry of Forestry and Water Resources, the Ministry of Transport Construction, and the Ministry of Ferrous Metallurgy with new, substantial additional expenditures and numerous organizational complexities. Only the fishermen stand to gain from it. It is enough for just one of these ministries to withhold its approval from a program——not refuse, just withhold——for the Council of Ministers not to review it at all. There are no conflicts in a socialist economy because according to theory there should not be.

An expert who knows the government bureaucratic mechanism said:

> We managed to block the construction of a highway around Baikal; that will at least save it from being overrun by tourists in their cars. We did this without the Council of Ministers, and that must be considered a major success. More serious proposals don't get to the Council of Ministers; some agency inevitably declares that they will inflict tremendous harm on its productivity——and that is it. . . . We cannot keep insisting. . . .
>
> Thus, even assuming that in the near future an All-Union Committee for Environmental Conservation is created, it will not be able to resolve the central, cardinal issues on an equal footing with everyone else. Ecological problems concern the whole society; and if society is going to be protected against poor decisions and the disasters that ensue, such a state committee must have real power. For this it obviously must be at a higher governmental level than the State Planning Committee or, at the very least, its equal as an opponent.

Despite the obviousness of such arguments, they will not be allowed to be enunciated in the Soviet press except as abstract comments on the ideas of foreign authors. It is even difficult for us to dream about the creation of a genuine system of ecological monitoring like the one at work, say, in Sweden.

But let's make one more supposition. Let's imagine that the planning system is changed and that there is effective ecological control. The experience accumulated by the courts and arbitration boards will find its reflection in new strict and economically sound laws. Let's suppose.

But for any law to go into operation it must rest on an appropriate philosophy, on people's clear convictions. What could support laws meant "to preserve nature for us and our heirs," as declared in the official press?

Why should the present generation of Soviet citizens give up a bit of their food? Compared with Western living standards, it is not all that abundant. Our society is concerned primarily with the satisfaction of material needs. And if there is some interest in our inner needs, it is only for the immediate, the transitory.

Do we have a real inner need for anyone, apart from our children and a few friends, to live better than we do, to enjoy the same beauty that has given us pleasure? . . . And not simply better, but at our expense. This detail would probably considerably narrow the ranks of enthusiasts for environmental conservation. More and more often people loudly declare that they don't want to live just for their grandchildren but also for their own children.

A student at the Higher Party School of the Central Committee of the CPSU told this story:

> We discussed this problem with our teacher. It is obvious that our society is ill prepared to sacrifice some of today's prosperity for the sake of remote and rather vague goals. We will not see the fruits of our present efforts, but for us communism is after all an insubstantial, blurry goal. We will not see it either. But if we don't want to be chatterboxes, don't want to waste words about communism, for which harmony between man and nature is an indispensable condition, we must set aside the means to preserve nature.

So the only argument in defense of nature is the authorities' unwillingness to be known as windbags, chatterboxes. But isn't this too tenuous? Isn't the purely rational argument that follows from the authorities' instinct for self-preservation sufficient? Hardly. In the near future the country's leaders may face even greater economic and political problems than those existing at present. To avoid discrediting themselves, it will be simpler to resort to other means than the fulfillment of difficult promises concerning preservation of the environment. Whoever could discredit the government when the mass media are 100 percent in its hands could attack anyone they wanted.

Either those who had once proclaimed the good conservation aims of a previous regime or those who inopportunely dared to recall those declarations.

In our profoundly materialistic society the spiritual links with the past, with our forebears, have been weakened to the extreme; and one can say that our frail spiritual bonds with our descendants are also almost completely lacking. The natural processes that man is disrupting now extend far in time beyond the frame of life of one or two generations. And laws on nature conservation will be effective if they accord with society's fundamental values.

In tribal society such value attached to the existence of the tribe, belief in the external transmigration of the soul, etc. In societies of the recent past they were provided, of course, by Christianity, Confucianism, Judaism, and other religions.

Pascal said, "The heart has its own reasons, which the human mind cannot comprehend."

One book on nature conservation in the USSR ends with the words of the medieval traveler Afanasii Nikitin: "No land is more beautiful than ours. The lord God has made it so."[7]

In another book the children's writer N. Sladkov describes in detail the customs of Indians who believe animals are sacred. He writes about religious India as a unique island of genuine reverence for life in the modern world.[8]

Not a single serious Soviet writer, whether communist or not communist, has found any moral basis for his appeals to save nature beyond somehow camouflaged religious doctrines. D. Rasputin, the author of the excellent novel *Farewell to Mother*, and V. Sapozhnikov, author of the documentary story "Operation 'Basin'" have turned to the idea of "God" or "the immortal spirit" in the face of a growing barbarism. They cannot find other absolute, nontransitory values.

The example of the Western countries provides no support for the illusion that the problems arising from man's disharmony with nature can be swiftly resolved through religious ideas. Clearly it is only through the development of profound, basic ideas about human existence that such a harmony, or at least the alleviation of disharmony, should be sought. But in our society virtually all spiritual literature, all modern philosophical literature, to say nothing of religious literature of various persuasions, is available to almost no one and cannot have any influence on social consciousness.

A hundred years ago George Kennan wrote that the absurd severity of Russian laws was diminished by half in the process of their chaotic enforcement. With regard to environmental protection laws, we can now say just the opposite: if all the laws needed for the preservation of the environment were introduced tomorrow, they would be enforced just as chaotically. On what support, aside from the personal virtue of a few enthusiasts, could they rely?

# 6 ...Swans Like The Winter Snows

Archpriest Avvakum wrote about Baikal: "So many birds. Geese, swans . . . upon the sea like the winter snows." The local peasants brought the archpriest a gift of forty fresh sturgeon.

Historical works contain a multitude of descriptions of how Rus abounded with wild beasts and birds.

. . . The myriad army of Ivan the Terrible lived on the meat of wild animals the entire way from Moscow to Kazan. Yet men still hunted then without firearms.

Just a century ago Przewalski bagged hundreds of pheasants a few steps from his bivouac in the Amur region at Lake Khanka. Only the pheasants' liver was taken for food.

A modern poet writes:

> With each year there are more airplanes,
> With each year, fewer cranes.

Today we would consider the hunting by the great traveler Przewalski amoral poaching. But Przewalski was not just a traveler; he was described by his contemporaries as a moral exemplar. That is what Chekhov wrote about him, and Chekhov must be trusted.

The fact was that until the end of the nineteenth century, even naturalists believed that wild animals should be either tamed or annihilated. The entire Christian world believed, without any sophistry, that God created man "to exercise dominion over the fishes of the sea, and over the birds of the heavens, and over the whole earth."

Changes began at the very end of the last century. In 1898 the exiled populist Iokhelson published a book in Petersburg in which he wrote about danger signs. He distinguished three kinds of hunters in the Siberian North. The first was the traditional local hunter, essentially a pagan; the second was the old Russian peasant entrepreneur who tries to profit from hunting but never kills animals senselessly and leaves breeding stock. The third kind is new folk without religious principles, who come for the season and kill everything in sight, even more than they can carry away and sell. They shoot animals not for money but for amusement, for sheer pleasure.[1]

This third, rapacious type has spread like the plague in the twentieth century. Neither the old Christian morality nor the new communist ideals make any impression on him.

Here is a quotation from a work written in 1976, seventy-eight years after Iokhelson's book:

"Powerful three-axle Gaza and Ural trucks, two LAZ and UAZ buses, plus our 'landrovers.' Eight vehicles. Our detachment resembled a military unit," recalls the author, the writer Vladimir Sapozhnikov, "not only with its large manpower and vehicle fleet—everyone was armed to the teeth. Cartridges on belts crossed bandit style, hacking knives, binoculars, flares. This 'mechanized army' could lay waste to the taiga with its hardware alone, but of course everyone also carried into the field his rifle, one or two barrels. Hundreds of barrels.

"I tried to estimate how many shots our 'army' would fire, how much wildlife they would kill, but I gave up: we were only one of hundreds of big-city enterprises going out today into 'nature's bosom.'

"In spring 1976 on Lake Chany in Siberia, ornithologists banded three hundred young ducks. In the fall they recovered all three hundred bands—every one of the banded birds had crossed someone's sight, been killed without a chance to breed."

Sapozhnikov goes on: "Just give hunters trained in galleries a chance, and they will turn everything that crawls, flies, breathes, and sings into a meal. . . ."

As Sapozhnikov describes it, "the bag limits were exceeded tenfold during the hunt. It was beautifully arranged brigandage, and a 'rapacious, cynical morality, the law of the Klondike on the hunting grounds.' But in the end someone noticed a V of swans. . . . And when it was far away, he sighed—a dream . . . it must be. . . . For the first time I see. . . .

"Someone's heart still trembled before beauty. Thank God!" concludes the writer.[2]

The invocation of God, in whom neither Sapozhnikov nor

certainly the callous hunters believe, is itself symbolic in its futility.

The country's hunting clubs officially number more than 1.1 percent of the total population, including infants. This is five to ten times more than in European countries. Actually three or four times more people, about six to eight million of them, own guns and go hunting. This is one out of every eight or nine male adults of all ages. This fully corresponds to the number of hunters in medieval society, where there were neither machines nor food factories, and the life of entire families depended on the meat of wild animals.

And despite such large numbers and substantial financial support, there are few places where hunting clubs actually enforce hunting regulations and breed animals and birds. In many regions, as for example in the Altai, such a club year in and year out takes into the forest only 10 to 15 percent of the feed allotted wildlife.

Eight years ago in Tadzhikistan a total ban on hunting was declared. It was a quite sensible step, but then the hunting clubs began to dismiss their huntsmen, and poachers destroyed birds and beasts on a greater scale than when hunting had been permitted. Within a few years of the ban over 40,000 guns had been sold; and after eight years had gone by, the hunting expert A. Kaletskii wrote about the danger threatening not just two or three animal species but the whole fauna of Tadzhikistan.[3]

In 1970 in the Khabarov District professional hunters alone bagged more than 5,000 roe deer, which was 7-8 percent of the entire population. In 1974 these hunters were able to take no more than a few hundred roe. The number of animals, it seemed, fell each year in direct proportion to the increase in the number of army divisions on the Chinese border.

In the army, which is better provided for than other groups of the population, poaching is one of the most popular pastimes. Law-breakers in uniform are always more difficult to catch and bring to account, since they can declare virtually any of their hunting activities a "strategic necessity." More than once game wardens in the Chita and Amur regions have stopped army trucks loaded with dozens of carcasses of stags, deer, and elk. But the wardens were powerless if the poachers had had time to stick a "radiation" label or a secret cargo sign on the truck body.

Eagles, hobbies, kites, and other birds of prey are wiped out from military helicopters just for practice. Ornithologists travel hundreds of kilometers over the open plains of Kazakhstan without encountering a single kestrel or hobby.

Local authorities officially commandeer military helicopters for winter wolf hunts.

The vital role of wolves in biocenosis has long been proven. In 1960 on the Taimyr Peninsula the hunting expert Michurin found that the wolf could not attain a speed above 80 kilometers per hour and sustain it for more than three to five minutes. Deer, even pregnant females, could all easily escape attack, except sick animals. After the mass wolf shoots, infectious diseases and worms in deer jumped from 2 to 31 percent.

Wolves are now being bred in the central regions of Russia. Yet local authorities and many ranking biologists still passionately believe that wolves cause tremendous damage throughout the country's sheep-raising areas. Behind such arguments usually lies the inability of collective and state farms to operate at a profit. The wolf pays with its skin for all the sheep sold "on the sly" or eaten. Only in fairy tales do wolves still decimate entire flocks of sheep——in reality the sheep flocks have long been devouring the wolves.

Invoking the threat of wolves, thousands of shepherds constantly carry guns and hunt the year round in the remote high-mountain regions that are now the last refuge for wild animals.

The very rare snow leopard and the common leopard in Azerbaijan, the hunting leopard and ibex in the mountains of Central Asia, and other animals listed in the Red Book are the most frequent victims of shepherds' bullets.

So simple a device, practiced in many countries, as compensating the collective farms for losses caused by predators has run into dozens of various difficulties here. And until it happens, predators are left practically defenseless in all areas not accessible to close supervision.

The killing of thousands of buffalo from which American trappers took only the tongues has become a symbol of human rapacity about which one can read in any Soviet book on conservation.

But similar incidents are going on right now on our own tundra and taiga. At river fords wild deer, defenseless in the water, are surrounded, shot, bludgeoned, and slaughtered. Dozens of carcasses are carried away by the current, but enough are left for the hunters, usually geologists, to eat their fill merely of tongues.

Hanging in the game warden's office in Tiumen Province is a photo: a blockage in one of the region's northern rivers. But it is caused not by logs but by the bodies of dead elk . . . Wild hunting barbarism has not disappeared with the advance of society. The wild animals *are* vanishing.

The lack of equipment and facilities for inspectorates monitoring the observance of hunting regulations is recounted in hundreds of sad anecdotes. The warden asks the poacher to give him a ride to the hunting area——he has neither car nor motor boat of his own——and promises in return to overlook the pillaging of this "nice" fellow and go after the others. And so on . . .

In summer 1977 *Pravda* published a biting satirical column: "Go Get Him, Warden." It describes poaching that had become almost legal in petroleum-rich Tiumen. The secretaries of the district committees and other local officials participated openly in illegal hunts.[4]

After the article was published, which also discussed the poverty of equipment of the wardens in comparison with the motorized poachers, the Main Hunting Administration of the RSFSR hoped to get at least a few patrol cars, boats, and snowmobiles (there are only a few in the entire RSFSR). In response, in 1978 the State Planning Committee of the USSR allocated two motorcycles . . . And at the Main Hunting Administration they drew lots to decide where they would be sent. In at least ten to fifteen other regions, the situation is no better than in Tiumen.

Of all institutions representing authority, the inspectorates to supervise hunting and fishing (the Fish and Game Services) are the poorest and worst-equipped with vehicles and other means of communication. Generally they neither have nor can they purchase the cars, boats, and vehicles commonly sold in stores to all hunters, to say nothing of helicopters or night-vision equipment that would sharply cut poaching.

The technological weakness of Soviet industry, which developed the capacity to produce snowmobiles (snowcats) fifteen years after American industry, saved the lives of thousands of denizens of the tundra and taiga over these years. Now that snowmobiles are being put out, there is practically no place in the entire north, from the Kola Peninsula to Chukotka, that remains inaccessible to hunters, for the machines go first not to wardens but to the hunters.

The steady growth of poaching in the country rests, apart from technical and administrative defects, on a solid economic base.

Meat, particularly fresh, top-grade meat, has been a rarity for many years in government stores in the industrial cities of Siberia, the Urals, and Central Asia. Poached elk, deer, and other wildlife have enjoyed and will continue to enjoy excellent sales.

Fur-bearing animals also bring good profits to poachers. The system of low government purchase prices is theoretically justified by the argument that since natural resources are owned by the people, the hunter does not consider the skins he takes his own property; he is just the supplier of these skins (a natural resource) to government purchasing stations. The hunters, of course, don't delve into these subtleties; they know that if they sell two fox pelts on the black market, they will get as much as they would get from the government for ten, and they behave accordingly. Almost every professional hunter meets the quota required of him and takes skins over it for himself. All this leads to overtrapping.

In recent years "innocent" physical measures, such as fenced cultivated pastures, have become, along with bullets and toxic chemicals, causes of animal death.

Cultivation begins with enclosure of territory in barbed wire —this has become a habit for people and almost understandable. Yet in Kalmykia the wire fences around pastures have caused the deaths of thousands of saiga antelope. The animals are killed as they crash into the fences at night while running at great speeds, either avoiding pursuit or simply in fright. The saiga also die in irrigation canals.[5] Three hundred saiga were picked off the wire fence in a single day on one state farm. They are now taking steps in Kalmykia to prevent repetition of such incidents, but the very fact shows how dangerous life has become for wild animals, how every day the chances grow of them falling into a trap set deliberately or unintentionally by man.

Whatever the situation on ordinary lands, our nature preserves have been set up by the government itself for the perpetual preservation of the entire wealth of flora and fauna.

Naturalists and biologists know an enormous amount about destruction of Soviet preserves by poachers as well as by state economic organizations.

The magazine *Hunting and Hunting Management* takes a principled stand on issues concerning preserves and reflects objectively—as far as that is possible under our conditions—the actual state of affairs.

Here are the titles of some articles that have recently appeared in the magazine:

"A Preservation Attitude for Preserves"
"Preserve—A Standard of Nature or a Logging Enterprise?"
"More on Logging Trends in Preserves"
"Preserve Problems Should Be Solved"
"The Sary-Chelek Preserve and Its Problems"
"More on the Problems of Sary-Chelek"
"Preserves and the Fishing Industry Are Incompatible"
"A Forest-Steppe Preserve Is Needed"
"The Kurgalzhino Preserve Needs Help"
And so forth—totaling more than thirty articles.

It is quite natural for an organ of the press to raise controversial issues and come back to them from time to time. But in this case it is not so much that *Hunting and Hunting Management* keeps coming back to the issues raised as that, judging from the texts of the repeated articles, after the first exposure there have been no improvements whatsoever. In a number of cases the violations of preserve regulations only grew worse in the interim. Generally both the first and subsequent publicity about flagrant violations of preserve conditions has had only a negligible effect. In the words of the magazine's editor, one can count no more than a few cases in which they substantively promoted nature conservation on the preserves.

Of the more than 100 (120 in the most recent tally) preserves that now formally exist in the country, one can count on one's fingers those about which articles have not appeared in the central or local press with impassioned pleas for help. There is no kind of economic activity that does not take place in these areas, where by law "all kinds of economic activity are prohibited," and the land is "withdrawn from exploitation in perpetuity."

At the Zakataly Preserve in Azerbaijan, a geological team began prospecting for oil without having requested formal permission from the management or even informing them.

At the Tigrovaia Balka Preserve in Tadzhikistan, cattle graze and there is hunting and fishing. To restore order on the preserve, the local authorities announced that after a certain date, a special brigade of collective farm workers, and not some random groups, as had previously been the case, would do the fish catching in the preserve lake.

At the Naurzum Preserve in Kazakhstan, a whole fishing business has been set up on the lakes, and dams have been built.

At the Kyzyl-Agach Preserve in Azerbaijan, a special fishing business has also been set up, with dams and canals crisscrossing its territory in many spots.

At the Sary-Chelek Preserve in Kirgizia, which retains its unique mountain nut forests, every conceivable type of economic activity goes on. In 1976 *Pravda* listed the infractions: cattle grazing, haying, hunting for wild animals, trapping them for sale, illegal nut gathering. Plus the devastation and cluttering of the land caused by masses of tourists.[6]

Each year the local authorities send telegrams to Moscow and the Main Administration for Nature Conservation and Preserves in the Ministry of Agriculture requesting that haying be permitted on the Sary-Chelek Preserve. Every year they make the point that this year it will be extremely difficult to gather feed (when in the past twenty or thirty years has it been easy?), and hence the succulent grasses of the preserve's forests and meadows will help dozens of collective and state farms and save thousands of head of cattle. The Main Administration, which is a part of the Ministry of Agriculture, cannot disregard livestock interests and each year accedes. As an exception . . . Dozens of collective farm brigades then descend on the preserve, and, of course, not only does the vegetation of the meadows suffer from the haying but so do the birds and animals in the forests. The walnut forests, where massive illegal nut gathering goes on, also suffer.

Cattle grazing and hay cutting are perpetual at the Aral-Kaigambar, the Turianchai, and the Kurgalzhino preserves. A few years ago, with immense effort, the warden, I. S. Sukhanov, and his deputy, Iu. L. Gorelev, managed to fence the Badkhyz Preserve against cattle grazing. But for how long?[7] The oldest preserve in the country, the renowned Askaniia-Nova, also suffers from cattle grazing and haying.

No outsider could ever guess that Issyk-Kul Lake and its entire shoreline is a nature preserve. Everywhere, with the exception of two or three places, cattle graze, settlements and roads are being built, and the dozens of existing beaches and resorts are being expanded. Countless fishing boats, freighters, and passenger vessels ply the lake.

The destruction of the very beautiful mountainscapes around Baikal caused by the swarms of tourists is causing serious alarm.The unplanned growth of tourism, like the growth of industry, is the reason why such formerly common birds as the common cormorant, the gray lag goose, the bean goose, the taiga swan-goose, and the great bustard are vanishing from Baikal. The white-tailed eagle, the black kite, the whooper swan, osprey, the bufflehead duck, the scoter, and other varieties of birds are on the verge of disappearing. On Olkhon Island, where huge flocks of sheep are driven for the summer, all the large animals have completely disappeared—elk, Caspian deer, roe deer, wolves, sable—as well as the birds—the cormorants and golden eagles. The shoreline of the island is littered with tourists—shreds of newspapers, plastic wrap, bottles, and cans pile up. In the heart of the island, three kilometers from the landing, a huge permanent trash dump has been built to which rubbish from the whole surrounding area is brought. Yet fifteen years ago Lake Olkhon was called one of the centers for the future Baikal National Park.

In the American national parks—Yellowstone and Yosemite—some serious problems have arisen in preserving the landscape in the face of an annual influx of six to eight million tourists. The valley of geysers in the Kronotsk Preserve on Kamchatka is visited by several thousand tourists every year; but with the way our tourism is organized, the entire valley is now endangered.

Local courts usually mete out very light fines for various infractions of preserve regulations. The most common penalty for poaching is a one- or two-year probationary sentence. But this means that, as before, the poacher stays home and hunts, but more cautiously. According to the testimony of the manager of the Lazov Preserve (Primorsk District), one malicious poacher, upon hearing the court's sentence of two years probation, threatened the preserve right in the court room: "I'll show them. They wanted to jail me. Now they'll see. . . ." Since that time each summer the preserve forests have burned in deliberately set fires; yet the police have shown no special interest in the man who made threats . . .

The annals of any preserve where wildlife is protected are replete with cases in which a ban on hunting has been violated by the very pillars of society, from the district level on up. This partly explains the lenient attitude of the authorities toward poachers.

Eliseev, the head of the Main Hunting Administration of

the RSFSR, once declared off the record that no one now hunted in the preserves in his system. Not even members of the Politburo . . .

There is no reason not to believe Eliseev or to doubt that this was a major achievement of the Main Hunting Administration. High-ranking officials do not hunt in the twenty preserves of the Main Hunting Administration—they hunt in the rest.

The Astrakhan Preserve in the Volga delta and the Ilmen Mineralogical Preserve in the Urals are two of the oldest preserves in the country whose founding decree was signed by Lenin himself. Since then nothing in particular has happened with the Ilmen Preserve (of course, the preservation of rare minerals was poorly organized; and while the stacks of the nearby industrial city of Miass smoke within legal limits during the day, at night, when no one sees, they belch out hundreds of tons of soot, dust, and sulfur, causing serious damage to the preserve's plant life). The Astrakhan Preserve has undergone a greater metamorphosis due to pollution of the Caspian and Volga, the decimation of bird life, and the cutting of reeds.

But now there is a different point. V. Kozlovskii, former head of the Department of Nature Preserves of the Main Nature Administration of the Ministry of Agriculture, used to tell in the late sixties about the government hunting expeditions that used to occur in the Astrakhan Preserve in the early and midsixties. Once, according to him, he was called to the preserve before the arrival of two of the country's leaders. When they arrived, he informed one of them, in full uniform, that the "territory of the Astrakhan Preserve had been withdrawn from economic use in perpetuity and that hunting of any kind was prohibited at all seasons of the year. . . ."

In response the leader said that he knew all that and would assume full responsibility . . . Procedure had been observed, and the hunt began! . . .

No ornithological conference, no symposium on fauna conservation ever takes place without mention of the Kyzyl-Agach Preserve on the shores of the Caspian to the south of Baku. This preserve is under the Ministry of Agriculture of the USSR; it has absorbed all the defects of the country's preserve system, absorbed and multiplied them many times over.

In 1971, at a conference of the International Organization for the Preservation of Wetlands for Migratory Birds in the Iranian city of Ramse, the shallow Kyzyl-Agach Bay (the official name of the bay is Kirov) and the local estuaries were named one of the most valuable refuges on the planet for migratory birds. More than three hundred species of birds, almost all those known in the USSR, gathered here either to winter or on migration. Flocks of mallards, teal, coots, etc., used to gather to winter in these warm regions, in some years numbering in the millions, in others, in the tens of millions.

On the other hand, Kyzyl-Agach Bay, shallow and warm, had in the past been so rich in sturgeon, perch, and carp that catches were even larger than on the celebrated crop banks of the Sea of Azov. The fantastic abundance of wildlife and valuable fish was also the reason for the constant pillaging of the preserve from land, sea, and air from the early fifties to the early seventies, when almost nothing was left to plunder.

The red-breasted goose is called the firebird. Even the ancient Egyptians were attracted by its unique beauty. They liked to depict it on their friezes and vases. Now the red-breasted goose has gone into the Red Book, and there are only two places in the world left where this bird, with its vermillion neck and grayish-blue plumage, can still be found: in the summer in Taimyr and in the winter at Kyzyl-Agach. Poachers have never been interested in the rare red-breasted goose, since the Kyzyl-Agach coot brings a much higher price on the market, and therefore it is killed only accidentally and one at a time. Nonetheless recently ornithologists have been unable to spot the red-breasted goose on the preserve. This fact alone provides some idea of the scale of hunting that goes on at Kyzyl-Agach.

Quite recently, now that the coot has become rare, the interests of the poachers have shifted. They have begun to kill the flamingo, which previously had been of no use to them; demand for its rose-colored feathers had emerged. Professor Mustafaev, the Baku ornithologist, told about the danger now threatening the flamingo in a letter to the Zoological Institute. According to legend, Kyzyl-Agach got its name from the flamingo: Kyzyl-Agach means rosy trees. And now even these beauties are abandoning the preserve . . .

The disgraceful plundering that reigns at Kyzyl-Agach has, as we said, often been discussed at the various conferences and meetings of biologists and naturalists; it was the subject of a good two to three dozen articles. The entry in the reference-publicity edition of *Preserves of the USSR* even mentions (the only such case out of almost a hundred preserves) the tremendous damage done to birds by mass hunting in motor boats.

The matter has been taken up repeatedly in commissions set up by the Central Committee of the Communist Party of Azerbaijan and the Central Committee of the CPSU. The preserve's manager was replaced, the directors of the local and republic fish services were changed, for a month or two order was reestablished, but then everything was back to "normal."

The economic reason that poaching flourishes has been the scarcity of meat in other parts of the country. Any amount of wildlife shot anywhere could be sold on the markets of nearby cities——Port Ilich, Lenkoran, Lerik——at top prices. The profits from black market trade in sturgeon and black caviar were even greater. Some idea of the size of the incomes of the illegal hunters can be gotten from the booming business done by their "firm" (no match for a government firm!). In the coastal village of Tazakend a hunter would sit in his motor boat almost at the very door to his house: special canals had been dug from the shore, and on the infrequent frosty days six or so fellows would break up the ice, keeping the canals in A-1 condition. The poachers' boats were equipped with two powerful motors, and the hunters carried two, even three double-barreled guns: the take of birds was put on a conveyor. Each day at dawn the cannonade began; around eleven oclock it quieted down a bit; by that time most of the birds were already being plucked in the backyards of Tazakend by the women and children; a few hours later hundreds of carcasses were on their way to the market in trucks . . .

The poachers paid a monthly tax to the management of the preserve (and so on up through the ranks: the police, the district executive committee, the district committee, and on to Baku). Yet this was only part of the lucrative firm called the "Kyzyl-Agach Kirov Preserve." The fishermen also paid their tax regardless for whom they fished——for the collective farm that had not fulfilled its plan or for themselves privately. Each boat plying the preserve bay had paid the impost earlier. (It was said that the tax was not at all exorbitant——only 20 to 30 percent of the catch.)

There was even a fee to get permission to graze sheep on the preserve steppe and in the Talysh foothills. Both the local collective farms and the private farmers who kept sheep were interested in the pasture. Sheep, fish, and wildlife——the gross turnover of the "firm" amounted to several million rubles per year. Obviously, with such incomes at stake there was little real chance of saving the preserve. At that time it had not been plucked to the bone. Now, in 1976-77, the bone is quite visible.

Apart from the economic factors and local customs, there was, and is, yet another circumstance that blocks putting things in order at Kyzyl-Agach.

Since the end of the forties Kyzyl-Agach has been favored by high-ranking military commanders for their hunting distractions. In other words, not only the poachers but the republic's and country's highest authorities were implicated in violations of the preserve.

The sport of high-ranking officials is not the only secret in the depradation of the preserve, but it was they who gave the whole system of pillage the solidity of a pyramid.

Hunting on the preserve is an extremely lucrative business for thousands of poachers; hundreds of local officials benefit from this activity, and moreover, they occasionally "frolic" on the preserves themselves; for dozens of high-ranking government officials hunting there is enjoyable. The pleasure lies in shooting on the richest land and also in another chance to see that the law was not written for them.

Stories about Marshal Chuikov's hunting expeditions in the Kyzyl-Agach have become a sort of folklore in the realm of nature conservation in Azerbaijan. In the late sixties Chuikov, at that time deputy chairman of the Council of Ministers for Civil Defense, came to Baku on the private train given him by the German Democratic Republic for "liberating the German people from fascism." Accompanying Chuikov were his companions in arms in the liberation of the Germans and a multitude of current friends and acquaintances. Early in the morning the marshal, his adjutants, and the entourage drove onto the preserve in a whole column of all-terrain vehicles. Communication cars and field kitchens brought up the rear . . .

First these valorous soldiers swept through the reeds along the bank of the inlet and shot at the ducks, geese, and teal to their hearts' content. Then the company went over to the shallow inlets and shot at the coots that usually gathered into dense black flocks.

Dozens, hundreds of these birds were knocked out of such flocks by the heavy fire. Somewhere in the roadless foothills the all-terrain vehicles would bog down; Chuikov left them, switched to others, and after a light snack, the third, main act of the marshal's hunting expedition began.

Chuikov transferred to a helicopter and, circling over the

reed banks and spotting a herd of wild boar, he began shooting at them with his automatic rifle. The marshal shot first, followed by a few of his subordinates.

Finally, at the "picnic" site, the trophies were laid out: dozens (or hundreds—who counted!) of coots and ducks, and fifteen or so boar, both sows and sucklings. In military operations with automatic rifle fire, the dead represent about one third of the total hit. Applying the same proportions to the hunting operation, one can probably assume an additional thirty boar had run wounded into the thicket soon to die.

At the very end of the hunt, which in sheer magnitude of shooting and imaginativeness (of weaponry, of course) went far beyond not only the hunting expeditions of the autocrat of all Rus but anything ever known in the hunting literature—at the very end tanks moved into the preserve. They were only there to tow out the stuck all-terrain vehicles; but even so one can say that every major kind of troop, with the exception of the missile men, participated in the marshal's hunt.

A few years ago an English film was shown on our screens in which a lunatic general hunted deer with ground-to-ground missiles equipped with heat-seeking warheads. Soviet zoologists and ornithologists commented ironically after viewing it that the English director and script writer must have really enjoyed making their little fantasy, which ridicules the maniac militarist. Among the divisions quartered in the Baikal area, however, hunting for deer in this manner has been a long and serious practice (in contrast to the pure fantasy of our Englishmen). Our rocket officers reasoned quite soberly that they could find no better targets for training troops to shoot ground-to-ground heat-seeking missiles at than wild boar and deer on the run. Startled by the sound of a shot, the animals dash across the wooded hills, and the accurate rockets overtake them wherever they go. Everything is quite logical, everyone sane . . .

Shortly after Chuikov's hunt, allusions to which had appeared in the press (in a satire in *Crocodile*), a sumptuous private house was built on the preserve grounds for prominent guests. It was put up on the shore of the bay, and it was said that the stone fence alone cost more than all the expenditures on scientific research at the preserve throughout the entire period of its existence since the early thirties. This blank fence surrounds a splendid park, a marble swimming pool, and the so-called guest house, faced in marble, for guests of the Azerbaijan government.

A special grand hunt (more grandiose even than Chuikov's?), to which the most prominent leaders from the fraternal Caucasian republics and from Moscow were to be invited, was proposed to celebrate the opening of the house.

For some reason the hunt never took place, but the house is never empty; and as marshals and other high-ranking officers had hunted at Kyzyl-Agach before Chuikov, so do they hunt there today. Of course, the game has become somewhat thinner, but then the comfort is greater. In February 1976 a helicopter landing site was constructed for the arrival of Marshal Grechko, the nation's minister of defense. It was so that he could spend just a few hours in the quiet groves of the preserve after his flight from the capital and change planes only once, from his jet to the helicopter.

At one time a journey to the southern Caspian, to Persia, was considered an event worthy of a whole book. It was still that way in the thirties. But now it is just a "safari," a common pastime. The hunt is becoming an indispensable symbol of luxury, style, just as Persian rugs once had been and a swimming pool at one's dacha is now. For influential hunters any point in the country is equally accessible. Even the polar icepacks.

Soviet biologists have made important contributions to the preservation of the polar bear in the Arctic, and their indignation was quite natural when they condemned the "white safaris" of wealthy hunters who killed the polar bears on the ice from American and Norwegian ships. But no Soviet author can publically voice his indignation about similar killings of bears by Soviet guns, by Soviet hunters. In the winter of 1976 the Archangel section of the Main Hunting Administration of the RSFSR, which is responsible for the Arctic sector, fined Marshal Batitskii, commander of the Strategic Missile Forces, for killing as many as fifteen polar bears. The bears had been shot like the boars at Kyzyl-Agach, from a helicopter, with an automatic rifle in a special turret. The fines totaled something on the order of 18,000 rubles, and in response the Economic Administration of the Ministry of Defense (not the marshal) transferred 4,000 rubles to Archangel. Then the case went to the Committee of People's Control of the Central Committee of the CPSU, which had already investigated the shooting of four bears the military could not deny. It was discovered that the animals, whose pelts lay at the fireplace in Batitskii's dacha, had been killed not by the master of the house, a passionate hunter, but by one of his adjutant colonels. This colonel had given the pelts to his commander, who saw nothing wrong in this, and who, busy with state affairs of "strategic (?) importance," suspected nothing.

The People's Control rebuked Batitskii nonetheless, saying he should have known where the skins of the vanishing polar bear came from, while the colonel was punished to the full measure of the law: he was relieved of his commission and expelled from the party.

The tragedy of Baikal continues; the Kyzyl-Agach hunting parties continue and get better. Despite a few positive achievements in preserving wild animals, one can say of them the same thing as of our forests: they are dwindling before our eyes. Of them one can say the same thing as of our clean water and our clean air.

In the destruction of the animals the moral factor, the psychology of total permissiveness and *"carpe diem"* plays no less a role than the economic advantages of poaching. Where our morals can ensure neither the inviolability of our preserves nor the survival of our wild animals, it is crucial that society have the example of moral behavior by its most prominent members, its leaders. Their respect for the law, for the idea of respecting all life could create a tradition of protecting wildlife. But do such people exist in our society? And would they be willing to give up their own whims?

# 7 New Technologies

"Why spend money sweeping the floors after work when people could just not litter?"

"The fundamental flaw in modern industry is clear: it is not only that its energy efficiency is on the whole less than that of a locomotive—2 to 4 percent—but that people must willy-nilly consume its wastes along with its useful products."

No one needs to be persuaded of simple truths like these—everyone agrees. When Academicians Petrianov and Semenov formulated possibilities for waste-free production, their articles were read with a sense of some relief: finally something radical had appeared in environmental protection. At least it was clear what had to be done.

A special session of the Academy of Sciences of the USSR recommended waste-free or, more accurately, low-waste technologies (production processes that generate absolutely no waste, particularly no loss of heat and energy, are impossible in principle), and their development was designated the general path for Soviet industry. It is waste-free technologies, not various trends in the development of treatment systems, that have been specified in several government resolutions as meriting the greatest attention and funding.

In theory industry uses all of Mendeleev's table; instead of people inhaling production wastes with the air and drinking them with their water, these wastes could be collected and channeled into other production, where they would be turned into something useful. Moreover, in a socialist economy, where everything is subordinate to the interests of society and not individual entrepreneurs, such comprehensive and ecologically untainted technologies could be developed much more rapidly than in a capitalist society. Soviet propaganda has written a great deal about "waste-free technologies" and about the advantages of socialism in their development.

Specialists who have to deal with the new technologies as part of their jobs have seen another picture.

Newspapers in all parts of the country have described the unique "First of May" chemical combine near Kharkov, which was supposed to produce chlorine and other chemicals without smoke or toxic effluents. A closer look showed that the official term "almost waste-free production" meant that it would pollute not the air or water, as usual, but the bowels of the earth. Concentrated liquid wastes from the combine were to be injected into deep layers of the earth's crust. Not long before this Academician Vinogradov said (and he was an eminent geochemist) that science had neither the means nor methods to prevent the gravest mistakes in selecting the strata and horizons for injection.

Nonetheless Vinogradov, vice-president of the Academy of Sciences, did nothing to prevent Academician Spitsyn from playing the same role with regard to the earth under Kharkov as Zhavoronkov had previously played with regard to Baikal. With Spitsyn's official scientific blessing, concentrated brines are now being pumped into the earth not only under Kharkov. They will be injected, for example, at the huge petrochemical combine on the shores of the Irtysh, which also, like the "First of May" combine, is billed as "waste-free production" without even the qualifier "almost."

In those cases in which waste-free production was achieved, no one wrote about the way——"from Moscow to Leningrad via Vladivostok"——it was done. One huge chemical plant in Krasnoiarsk Territory, which produced polyethelyne film, had by 1975 become an excellent example of how to turn "effluents into income." Since its opening in 1968 the plant had emitted huge quantities of fluorine into the atmosphere, and the taiga had withered over a radius of several kilometers. Since its opening the plant engineers were aware that the best way to protect the atmosphere was to recover the fluorine and sell it to other enterprises where fluorine was in short supply. To implement this uncomplicated and in all respects advantageous idea took more than five years, while thousands of hectares of taiga were ruined, and its supporters suffered heart attacks pushing it through myriad agencies. At the plant there was no one who didn't note ironically: "If we had a private firm, the owner would have sold the fluorine from the very first day."

Most likely the owner would have made some adjustments even in the planning stage, worrying about his own advantage and about observing the environmental protection laws.

In this instance the situation was complicated by the fact that the production of fluorine and polyethylene come under different administrations in the Ministry of the Chemical Industry. Neither the fact that both agreed in principle that raw material had to be processed totally, efficiently, nor the fact that both administrations were in the same ministry building on neighboring floors changed anything. Each administration had first to do the job for which it had been created—fulfill the plan for a certain volume of output. Many years are spent solving problems having no bearing on this primary task.

The matter is drawn out even longer when different ministries are involved in planning new multiple production processes. The end is not in sight for the "tug of war" over the multiple use of resources in Kar-Bogaz-Gol Bay on the Caspian Sea or the apatite-nepheline ores of the Kola Peninsula. What goes into the dumps at the Khibin mines contains large quantities of nepheline, a valuable raw material for the aluminum industry. But the Ministry of Nonferrous Metallurgy does not want to spend millions building a concentrating mill (this would lower the plan indices for the performance of the entire ministry for several years), nor does the Chemicals Ministry want to do so. Any combine they built to process tailings would not be reflected in any of the major plan indicators—why should the ministries make the effort? For a laudatory newspaper story? Hardly a powerful incentive when the issue is spending millions, and the risk is losing one's job if the plan is not fulfilled. And while for ten years negotiations have been going on, the aluminum raw materials have not simply been stockpiled; no, for some reason they have been dumped into Imandra Lake! Meanwhile by-product valuable elements are not extracted from what is supplied to phosphorus fertilizer plants, and millions of tons of metals "forgotten" by industry are spread over farm lands.

The new thermoelectric power plants of the Ekibastuz District will emit 140,000 tons of ash per day within a few years. Enormous ash heaps bury thousands of hectares of land and are becoming a genuine disaster for the local inhabitants. Some of the waste is excellent raw material for the same aluminum industry, and a resolution to build a pilot plant was signed by the ministries of energy, coal, and nonferrous metallurgy in 1971. Since then not one nail has been hammered nor one brick laid at the site.

Not long ago a new technology applying steam and water was adopted in extracting sulfur in Byelorussian mines. In the process the mines emit effluents containing as much as 50 to 60 milligrams of hydrogen sulfide per liter of water. Another technology for extracting sulfur has been developed——it is water-free, using 1,000- to 2,000-kilowatt electric generators. Such generators are not a technological problem; but since up to now industry has not needed generators with greater capacity than 630 kilowatts, they were never produced. Hence negotiations to produce the new generators have dragged on for several years.

In Turkmenia water is trucked dozens of kilometers to the sulfur mines, but even this has not budged the matter from the sticking point. "Who benefits?" Since the days of Rome, lawyers have made this one of their first questions: he who benefits is most likely to do the "deed." He who benefits, he who obtains the material or moral advantage, is also the one most likely to find a way to solve a production problem. Who benefits from the adoption of an ecologically clean method using generators instead of the "dirty" method of superheated steam and water? Actually no one, although the generator method is only one third as expensive. The mine? The criterion for its performance is not profit but the plan; hence cheapness is of little concern. Whatever benefit the mine might get, it can only request that the generators be supplied; it has no right to seek funds to order generators, pay a bit more for them, and then return the money, and so on. The main administration? Its job is to worry about cheaper production; but since the plan is fulfilled all the same, its zeal goes into writing letters: "Speed up the production of generators," and the like. In every ministry, including that for chemicals, there is now a department of environmental protection; it is concerned with the interests of nature, regardless of the plan. And the "conservationists" do not sit there with hands folded, although they have no power to offer material incentives to or punish those who break laws concerning nature——indeed, they have no power at all. They can only recommend the same thing: "Speed up the production of generators." No one has special interests, nor can anyone "get rich" from the new technology. Here the principle of a socialist economy operates starkly.

The situation with the sulfur-extracting technology at the Byelorussian mines is even more absurd than it appears at first glance. The hydrogen sulfide mine effluents run into a river in the Vistula Basin. It turns out that Byelorussia is polluting Poland through the head waters of its principal river. To stop this more than a million rubles were earmarked for a canal that would carry the waste waters into our own Dniepr. But why wasn't it spent for the generators that would have solved the problem at its roots and recouped all the costs?

In the press and in conversations, engineers and rank-and-file scientists ask many questions that bear notably on the destruction of rivers, wildlife, or rare plants but also on an economic system that does not ensure environmental protection in general. They say that the rates for reclaiming land should be raised. Given the present low rates for reclaiming projects, which require a great deal of labor and equipment, very little is added to the gross cost of fulfilling the plan for a mine or quarry. If it is more advantageous for a quarry to do other projects than reclaiming, then even if reclamation efforts are provided for in the plan, they are not made under some pretext. To interest an enterprise it is necessary to estimate the labor cost of restoring land not on the basis of labor expended, as is now done in almost all cases, but on the basis of the social value of the restored lands.

Experts say that our system of planning indices is now such that in most cases it is of no advantage to an enterprise to adopt a new technology whatever its technical or ecological merits! They also say that it is disadvantageous for construction organizations to have anything to do with installing various treatment systems because their start-up dates are continually missed. Furthermore, it is of no advantage to builders to start up industrial enterprises ahead of schedule, even by one day. They also say that many plan indices work directly against industrial development and against technological progress. The status of the economy is a special topic, but where it touches on ecology a general fact can be noted.

Despite the development of new low-waste technologies, one of the top officials of the Ministry of the Chemical Industry confessed that the accumulation of wastes and the growth of dumps at chemical plants not only were not decreasing, they were even accelerating. They represent 6 to 10 percent per year, and in terms of weight, the tailings have already gone from millions to billions.[1]

As long as enterprises have no real economic interest in ecologically clean technologies, forcing them to adopt such processes is more or less like forcing a cat to eat cucumbers by giving it a lecture on the benefits of vegetarianism.

Even the strictest laws fail without economic reinforcements. On May 16, 1974, the Ministry of Water Resources, the Ministry of Health, and the Ministry of Fishing adopted new rules for the protection of surface waters. Specifically, they categorically prohibited the start-up of any enterprise that would discharge pollutants of unknown toxicity, i.e., those for which health experts had not yet set maximum permissible concentrations. Since then plans for plants that would discharge new, unknown substances have not been approved. Everything, it seemed, was fine. But as long as industry continues to develop through the synthesis of new substances previously unknown in nature, plants will continue to be built to produce them. Health experts have not been allotted one kopeck more money to determine maximum permissible concentrations for new pollutants; and since their quota remains a few dozen standards per year, they set that many, although each year chemists produce hundreds of substances. (Here is where research through the Stanford Program would come in handy, but our government wouldn't go along!) As a result particularly important—strategic—chemical facilities are still being built despite the new rules. It is not impossible that little by little less important and less urgent facilities will also begin to be built, since even if they had the money, health experts could not immediately make up lost ground and publish hundreds of new MPCs.

At the end of any article or any interview on environmental conservation issues, one finds the figure eleven billion rubles. That is how much was allocated in the period 1975-80 to nature conservation in our country, including the development of waste-free technologies.

The figure sounds impressive enough. But is it enough to rectify matters or even maintain nature in its present state? Of the dozens of people concerned with ecology, it would be hard to find even one who actually shares the enthusiasm of columnists about this sum. More often they say that it is actually rather small although it is something. Sometimes the comments on these eleven famous billion have been quite ironic.

"Eleven billion?" asked an economist dealing with questions of ecology. "That is a bit over two billion per year. We take that much from nature gratis—or more bluntly, do that much damage—in a month. But on top of that, it is so spread over various agencies—the right hand, as usual, does not know what the left is doing—that it is a wonder that they haven't done more harm, the eleven billion, than good."

"You say eleven billion spread over the agencies," sneered a skeptical naturalist. "Well, of course, the greater part of this, as usual, is chucked to defense agencies."

"Do you know the best proposal for using the eleven billion?" asked a third. "Use them to float all the wood sunk in the rivers and lakes. First, the rivers would become cleaner; second, some of the lumber, seasoned oak, could be sold for foreign exchange; and most important, none of the billions would cause any damage to nature."

# 8 New Ideas

*"Our situation is not generally better than theirs, that is, in the United States or in Europe," confessed Academician N in a conversation about the ecological crisis. "But for them everything ahead is black, while for us there is at least theoretically a ray of hope."*

What are these theoretical advantages?

Most Soviet ecologists believe that science undoubtedly provides opportunities to solve the main problems, but that because of economic difficulties society is in no position to realize the potential. And speaking frankly, it is not clear when it will be. Because they want to stay honest, yet at the same time because they fear conflicts with the authorities, many Soviet specialists postpone total solution of ecological problems . . . until communism. Until the day when at a wave of the hand, all the difficulties of economic growth and all political and national problems will dissolve in an ideal society. Such a position is very handy for outright political calculations as well.

At the ecological conference in Pushchino, B. Iusupov, a chemist from Ufim, and Khomentovich, a corresponding member of the Academy of Sciences, commented worriedly that the practice of pumping toxic and concentrated wastes into deep strata of the earth was becoming a dangerous "fad" in Bashkiria. Speaking after them, F. A. Gismatov, also from Ufim and a specialist in scientific communism, declared that "a better nature is not in the past but in the future"! Why? Where will it come from? That is not important. What is important is a declaration of principle.

In dealing with ecological problems many scientists understand perfectly well that finding a solution to many of them is unrealistic within the framework of science alone. They are also quite aware that their recommendations have a negligible influence on the authorities' economic and social decision-making. If he takes a sober view of things, the scientist can only concentrate on his purely scientific problems and not interfere in "their practical implementation, in how they are handled."

The well-known ecologist Academician S. S. Shvarts related at one conference how huge pines were growing on the grounds of his institute of ecology, not very far from the superindustrial zone of the Urals. One of them had reached sixty meters in height, but no signs of degradation were evident either on it or on its neighbors. Of course, this very tree had been cut down.

"But," said Shvarts, "it died of bad management, not the influence of industry."

"But isn't this an indicator of industrial development?" asked someone in the audience. "For example, in the Baikal region poachers can kill deer and roe deer outright because there is no meat. It's all the same to the deer or to your pine what factor impacts on them——normal development of society or abnormal. . . ."

"That isn't science——it's poaching," interjected a scientist. "It's not fit to discuss."

Until they intersect the system of management, pure science and its applied branches have a quite active life as regards ecological problems. All sorts of information on various local and technical aspects of pollution are more widely disseminated in scientific circles. The number of bulletins and newsletters of every conceivable sort is growing in all branches of industry—— from ferrous metallurgy to hydraulic engineering. Ideas are being generated that are of indubitable interest to the public. Some of them could substantially alleviate and blunt the acuteness of the crisis processes.

In a little information pamphlet the Lvov researcher Tupytsia and his Leningrad colleague Petrov provide a concise and clear analysis of the economic and ecological problems of the "Russian forest." Without depending on the warm and convenient dream of communism, these scientists propose some realistic ways out of the disastrous situation.[1]

Just how disastrous the situation is is evident from mass publications. Iu. Shaporev writes in the *Literary Gazette* that the modern logging industry destroys as much forest as do fires. And 200,000 to 300,000 square kilometers are burned in the

USSR ever year, with these areas growing steadily. "Will the Mountain Altai ever again be clad in forests," asks Shaporev, "if 80 to 90 percent of all the seedlings in these areas either die or produce merely scrub growth?"[2]

In Primor'e Territory the priceless Korean cedars are being cut for export; but because of the poorly coordinated transport system, the Japanese buyers reject most of the lumber, which does not suit their specialized production. This timber could be used, of course, for ordinary purposes, but the paradox of the planning system in this instance is: the expensive cedar lumber heats the furnaces of Ternei Region.[3] Cedars are being felled around the Sikhote-Alin Preserve, thereby directly threatening the ecological balance on the preserve. According to the testimony of one of the preserve workers, cedars will never grow again on these barbarous clearings, many hillocks are left completely bare, while in the valleys grow puny groves fit for nothing.

In a curious note that somehow got into *Pravda*, A. P. Kitaev, director of the Pokhvistnevskii Logging Enterprise in Iaroslav Province, admits in passing that in the ten years he has worked there, the management has never questioned him about fulfillment of the plan for replanting seedlings, but only about the plan for fellings.[4] This in a forestry enterprise whose purpose is to plant forests, not cut them.

The innumerable similar, quite distressing examples given by Tupytsia and Petrov boldly spell out the economic components. They show that the current situation in the timber industry cannot ensure:

1. the reproduction of the forest;
2. the multipurpose use of lumber in the economy;
3. the profitable functioning of most forestry enterprises.

They cannot do so for specific economic reasons. As a result the level of mechanization in the forest industry is declining, personnel turnover is increasing, while the level of qualifications is decreasing. Those who work in the forestry industry are becoming disinterested and impartial observers of "the fate of the Russian forest." (As we see, the conclusions of economists fully accord with the conclusions of the jurist who observed the demise of hundreds of thousands of cubic meters of lumber at the camp near Krasnoiarsk.)

The fundamental evil, say the authors, lies in the obsolete price system. They propose a switch to a new one and show that this need not lead to an increase in the prices on finished wood products, since expenditures on working the forest should simultaneously diminish. The new price system will interest enterprises in fully processing branches, bark, sawdust, and other by-products. Moreover, it also takes into account the fact that a forest is not only wood but also a producer of oxygen, a "producer" of many other benefits, including esthetic ones. Studies done in Sverdlovsk show that under present economic conditions, logging is the worst way to exploit forests. In the Urals, for example, a hectare of forest produces oxygen that is 45.2 times greater in value than what is obtained for its wood! Forest fees do not take into account either the oxygen, the climatic, or the soil conservation factor of forests.

The effectiveness of the new guidelines proposed by Tupytsia and Petrov has been demonstrated in practice in the United States and Sweden, but they would certainly not lead to the intrusion into socialism of market economy methods or other "capitalist heresies." Nonetheless, as the authors themselves acknowledge, it is too soon to count on their implementation in our forestry industry. In ten years . . . That is, when even more tens of thousands of square kilometers of irreplacable cedar, larch, and pine forests have disappeared.

In his book *Science and Survival* Barry Commoner has shown that the introduction of aluminum as a building material and the use of aluminum foil in packaging and other areas where it could be easily replaced has been very harmful for the environment. At all stages—from extraction to smelting—the production of aluminum generates toxic fluorine and other pollutants and consumes fifteen times more energy than the smelting of steel. The mass consumption of aluminum has become a fact because it gives firms a greater advantage than steel.

At a symposium at Leningrad State University, similar studies based on official Soviet statistics were discussed. The upshot was similar: the widespread use of aluminum is ecologically absurd. Like the Americans, Soviet consumers must consider whether they want to have goods packed in foil at the price of forests withered by fluorine. Or be able to buy lightweight chairs, loungers, and other trivia at the price of building the new thermoelectric power plants that are necessary for aluminum production and that will pollute both the air and the water. No other way to produce aluminum yet exists, and the desire to maintain our health dictates above all else a choice: we are going to have to give up all minor and trivial conveniences.

The Soviet researcher went further than Commoner; he studied the industrial use of all pure substances, primarily metals. Copper, mercury, arsenic, and cadmium. They do not exist in pure form in nature, just as nature knows no pure colors in its creations. In nature the ores of heavy metals are found in isolated "pockets" in the lithosphere. Man extracts them with great difficulty and, after expending tremendous efforts to do so, uses them for ephemeral ends. Later they cause and will continue to cause him greater harm than the most foul organic wastes. Since organic material sooner or later decomposes, the pure substances and the compounds they form will continue to poison life until they are isolated again somewhere in the deep "pockets" of the earth's crusts.

There is no need to go far for examples. The Soviet reader probably heard about cadmium only after it had caused a terrible disease in Japan, when the wastes from a factory got into the drinking water.

Geochemists studying samples of snow and soil in Moscow's Filei District found antimony and cadium concentrations occasionally exceeding the norm 100 times. According to reports of medical scientists, the presence of cadmium sharply increases the morbidity rate for viral influenza in the capital.

The purpose of studying pure substances in ecology is not to turn "progress back"; it is an attempt to point out the fundamentally antiecological nature of procedures that increase and increase the use of pure substance and heavy metals. It demands caution and deliberation in developing new technologies.

In contrast to Commoner's works, and even those of Tupytsia and Petrov, this report did not see the light even in pamphlets "for official use." The hundreds of specialists whom it might have jogged into reflection, new ideas, and approaches know nothing about it.

The USSR is in a better position with regard to the ecological crisis than the countries of the West. It has not gone as far here, and most important, it started later. Why then are there usually neither journals for publications nor time at conferences for serious probing of Western mistakes and lessons, for discussion of our own efforts? Why should socialism fall into major ecological errors step by step after the West?

The very fact that socialism so consistently repeats these errors suggests that, perhaps, there is no other way.

As in the West a few years ago, the press in the USSR is

now portraying atomic energy as the main hope for the near future. In the United States, Sweden, and other countries, many of the ecological hazards of atomic power plants have now been perceived; but Soviet propaganda blithely ascribes all this to the "organic defects of capitalism." From newspaper articles to the serious forecast *Nature 1990*, the building of atomic power plants is portrayed as the solution to both energy and air pollution problems. Nothing is even said about the profound doubts engendered by atomic power plants. The skeptics and opponents of atomic power plants are not given a single page in the press.

Yet their objections are no less serious than the objections of their Western confederates. Moreover, there are also some specifically Soviet factors.

A few hundred kilograms of uranium for an atomic power plant instead of thousands of tons of coal——this seems very attractive. But to get these few kilograms, thousands of tons of ore must be mined. The dumps of radioactive rock will be eroded by the rain, scattered by the wind, significantly and extensively polluting the environment. To concentrate uranium requires thousands of tons of sulfuric acid, and this is one of the "dirtiest" production processes. An atomic power plant needs pure graphite, zirconium, beryllium, cadmium, nickel, and ultrapure sodium. None of this is cheap from the ecological viewpoint. The atomic power plant is the next quirk in the technologies that have brought the world to ecological crisis. Before it even produces one kilowatt of energy, an atomic power plant is more costly to the natural environment than all other forms of energy production. Even with the most modern treatment equipment, strontium and cesium escape from the stacks of atomic power plants. Their quantities are a million times smaller than the amount of carbon monoxide or sulfur dioxide that now swirls around any thermoelectric power plant. But the hazards posed by strontium and cesium for man, birds, and fish are incomparably greater.

Claims that the burial of radioactive wastes is a problem only for the West seem baseless. The USSR had the sad experience of an explosion of nuclear wastes in 1958 near Cheliabinsk, when all crops, all animals, and houses were destroyed, and the population was evacuated 200 and more kilometers from the point of the explosion. It was only chance that the radioactive cloud did not reach Sverdlovsk but passed over a comparatively sparsely populated region. The number of victims remains a secret to this day.

Not even specialists can get their hands on more neutral data, for example, the economic indices of the performance of atomic power plants. As a result many assertions concerning the benefits of atomic energy cannot be verified.

Nor can ecologists check the reliability of current methods of burying wastes. It is clear, however, that they are very complicated and costly. Hence it is natural to expect that with the broad development of atomic power plants, methods of protection and waste burial will be made simpler and cheaper at the expense of safety.

Only one thing is sure: the development of atomic power plants accords with the strategic interests of the government, the interests of the military. As in other cases, this is the main reason that no objections can be found even in the classified press. However, there is a tried and true method to placate public opinion—appeal to authority. To the current Zhavoronkov, who in the realm of atomic energy is Academician Styrikovich. No matter what he says, in each instance the word "academician" is the main argument in support of his point of view. An academician is a unique higher assay of the gold of truth. Or rather of what propaganda puts out as gold and as truth.

"The views of Soviet scientists on the development of atomic power plants were unanimous and positive," said a Soviet ecology policy-maker, A. Ananichev, member of the Committee on Science and Technology. So it was until President Carter's energy program appeared in spring 1977.

The arguments of their American colleagues could not shake the Olympian objectivity of the views of the scientists around Styrikovich, although scientific truth was somewhat amended immediately after the political steps taken by the American government.

Relatively recently William Douglas presented the development of thermonuclear research in the USSR as an example to the American government.

"The Russians," he wrote, "supported by their government, are leading in the study of this cleanest form of energy and in 1978 plan to construct the first magneto-hydrodynamic generator, with a capacity of 1,500 megawatts. They are five to ten years ahead of the United States."[5]

In the summer of 1977, at a conference in the Novosibirsk Academic City, specialists from the Kurchatov Institute reported that the magnetic hydrogenerator would not be put into operation. Its construction had not been begun because there was no money for it. By now the United States has caught up with us and, evidently, will overtake the USSR in this field, since their magnetic hydrogenerator projects have been guaranteed financial backing for many years ahead.

Funding of the development of solar energy, the cleanest and ecologically soundest form of energy, has fared no better. In 1965 William Douglas remarked, when shown some solar batteries, heaters, and pumps in Tashkent, that greater achievements than this were to be found nowhere in the world.[6] But ten years later, in 1975, visitors to the Tashkent institutes were being shown the same outstanding solar equipment, and no more of it was to be seen anywhere: industry had been unable to put it into production.

Solar energy could supply 15-20 percent of the total energy needs of Central Asia if it were given sufficient attention and funds. Fifteen percent is not trivial, especially considering the ecological situation in Central Asia—many geologists attribute a "side issue" like the severe earthquakes in Uzbekistan to the rapid depletion of natural gas supplies.

Of all the ecological studies in the social sciences and economics, only the works of Academician Fedorenko's fellow economists enjoy official support. Professor M. Ia. Lemeshev and his assistants proposed that a "pay for pollution" system be introduced. In this system an enterprise must include in the net cost of its product the value of natural resources spoiled, measured by the cost to restore them. This damage should be made one of the indices of an enterprise's performance, and then every factory would have an economic interest in consuming as few natural resources and despoiling the environment as little as possible in its production process.

In many respects such a system, if it were to be adopted by the State Planning Committee, could bring about some positive changes in environmental protection. Critics, however, have pointed out that such an incentive mechanism for preserving nature by means of product price regulation would be too complicated and would inevitably function poorly.

More serious objections to Lemeshev's system are ethical. In a "pay for pollution" system it will be advantageous for an enterprise to treat its emissions into the atmosphere or water only when the harm done to nature and to the health of the population exceeds the cost of the treatment equipment. Hence there is a very real possibility that if gas emissions harm mainly old age pensioners or children or cause no noticeable disruptions besides miscarriages (as was actually the case in 1973-74 in one Vladivostok district), then the additional health expenditures in that area will be low, and the factory will have no reason to install expensive treatment systems. The early death of pensioners could even represent a saving for state insurance funds.

A factory's interest in cleanup will also depend on what kind of product it puts out. A producer of scarce and expensive metals could tolerate more chronically sick people near it than a factory producing ordinary goods.

Pricing all the natural resources on which the health and life of people depend in rubles makes it necessary to evaluate human life itself in rubles.

At a conference in Tbilisi in 1976, someone suggested to Lemeshev, one of the authors of the "pay for pollution" system, that he carry it to its logical conclusion and determine how much one human being was worth.

"That's not hard," answered the director of the Hydrometeorological Service of the USSR, corresponding member of the Academy of Sciences, Iu. Izrael, for Lemeshev. "It's not hard to determine from per capita national income."

Our national income is known to be about $2,000 per capita, but this figure was never heard in the big auditorium. Izrael remembered in time that U.S. national income was two times bigger— $4,000 per capita—and this would mean that one American was worth two Russians. Izrael quickly changed the subject.

One of the enquiring professors found himself on the other side. He nonetheless decided to test Lemeshev's ideas. He proposed that each of the respected members of the conference arbitrarily set a value on his own life and then the life of the comrade sitting next to him. The difference, claimed the professor, would be more substantial than the difference in the national incomes of the United States and the Soviet Union.

Well, say our national income was $4,000 per capita, and the American, on the other hand, was $2,000. Would you then, Professor Izrael, price each and every one of us in the ledgers of the State Planning Committee at $4,000 per capita?

Then we could also boast that a Soviet citizen was the most valuable species in the world.

The discussion at Tbilisi touched only purely theoretical questions, and even those, thanks to Izrael's alertness, did not go very far. But the changes taking place in the consciousness of contemporary scientists and politicians is indicative. It is indicative of erosion in humanistic views and their replacement by a perception of man as a sum of all the material and nonmaterial goods produced and consumed by him.

The nihilism and denial of the immortal human soul that were the source of Dostoevsky's tragedies have assumed new "theoretical" forms in our mass society.

It is not the first time that attacks on the dogma of the infinite worth of the human individual have appeared in the pages of our press. Ten years ago the famous surgeon Amosov proposed that the notion of the infinite worth of human life be rejected when a patient's death is a confirmed fact, and that permission be given to remove his organs for transplantation in other patients.[7] The "divine" notion of a priceless individual was a definite hindrance in such a case.

Then the mathematician Iu. Shreider, in an article in *New World*, demonstrated the implications of a morality imposed by concern for patients. He drew perfectly logical conclusions from the proposition that the value of the human organism was just as calculable as the value of a complex machine: ". . . to repair a more expensive machine we always dismantle a less expensive machine for parts. To save the life of an outstanding academician, we should sacrifice the life of an ordinary student. . . ."[8]

In this case the calculation is of the sort: are the lives of X, Y, or Z worth installing an expensive "clean" technology in the factory near their homes? Or should we install an imported "clean" technology near the house of so key and socially useful a worker as Academician N or Marshal M? Or of a dozen hard-to-replace workers in some unusual profession?

In practice such a choice is made daily, secretly, and of course, not in favor of the ordinary people X, Y, and Z. Nonetheless it has so far been hushed up as a deviation from officially accepted standards. Theories setting a price on vital goods and on the human individual——which include Lemeshev's suggestions——can erode the basis of science and trivialize standards. The humanistic ideals of society are being impugned by economists precisely at the point where our mass consumer society is least able to defend itself.

In unofficial and semiofficial conversations, viewpoints are regularly expressed that diverge substantially from propaganda aims. The semiofficial sociologist-futurologist I. Bestuzhev-Lada even ventures to talk about ecologically justified zero growth of industry and zero population growth, i.e., he shares the ideas of the Club of Rome, although he relegates this zero growth to some remote future, probably to the era of communism.

The leadership of the Committee for Science and Technology and the Academy of Sciences may invite members of the Club of Rome to unannounced meetings in Moscow and have affable conversations with them. This changes nothing in the course of our ecological policy and most likely will continue to change nothing.

"In the late '80s and early '90s we should expect some very serious ecological situations," declared in a lecture A. Ananichev, an expert on ecological policy. "Situations that will shake all industry and society and force us to take emergency measures, to reexamine the ecological problems of the economy and reject many former complacent notions."

The catastrophe will not burst upon us in a day. Fate is rather good to mankind, and the horrors described by the prophets of an ecocollapse will most likely not befall mankind in one or two years but will extend over two or three generations. They will be somewhat less horrible. The poetic time in which the awesome prophets of Israel lived, and in which modern antiutopian writers live, is a compact and condensed time. Biology and evolution have their own time, and the ecological catastrophe will probably approach as a series of emergencies, on the installment plan, as it were.

But basically this changes very little. Measures taken in emergency situations are unique in their abruptness and totality. It is not hard to comprehend what lies behind Ananichev's admonitions about critical future situations even for socialist society, behind his allusion to a reexamination of "complacent notions."

The position taken by our country's leaders is one of observing the development of the ecological crisis. They have neither the desire nor the means to take any serious steps against the crisis, since those steps could lead to major changes in the economy and moreover in the management of production and the system of power. "If thunder doesn't rumble, the peasant doesn't cross himself." But if the thunder does roll, then even with different leaders, they will cross themselves. And once the thunder has boomed, then any abrupt measures will seem justified. The passive position of our "higher-ups" is not surprising; but for society a prospective reorganization under the pressures of all kinds of shortages of the most vitally necessary resources will threaten to turn it into a sort of "brave new world." Into a society where the freedom of the individual and the full development of his capacities will not be an issue even on paper, perhaps because then there won't be spare paper, just as there won't be any "spare" resources. The entire life of society will be regulated, like the flow of all rivers; and the consumption of even such long shared resources as clean water or the peace and calm of a remote forest preserve will be strictly limited for its members.

Whether it be the gloomy forecasts compiled by futurologists, or the equally gloomy sentiments fermenting among economists who propose measures against impending economic disasters or, among ecologists, against impending ecological catastrophes—all this reaches our public (not on its own, of course, but through propaganda media) in the form of a kind of "spring stirring." "Spring" since if we *do* have problems, they are "the problems of growth and are easily resolved."

This is the way propaganda represents the matter; and without the means to get information of another sort, the majority of the population thinks this way or about the same.

Those initiated into the "secrets of the Russian water, earth, and air" think otherwise. "Our relations with nature are afflicted by the same ailments as in capitalist countries, plus an ignorance of how far these ills have gone," is the way one expert formulated his point of view. "Accordingly, we cannot even apply all the necessary remedies."

The lack of public knowledge is a well-known flaw in our system. But is public knowledge really necessary in the realm of environmental protection?

What is the point of endlessly intimidating people with the specter of ecological catastrophes? Why does Western propaganda shatter the nerves of a people already exhausted? Can ordinary citizens really do anything to help those experts, trustworthy and reliable people, whom the government has assigned to deal with ecology? A doctor does not tell the truth to a patient with cancer; but if there is a possibility of saving him, he does so.

Such doubts about the need for the broadest public forum for eco-information is the professional demagogy of those who have made the totally controlled information media a profitable business for themselves.

For society the situation can no longer be useful when decisions about a major ecological project are made by two or three "leading" comrades, while the "strategic" reasons that guided their selection of the project remain unknown to millions whose lives will be substantially affected by it. And even if it is discussed in scientific councils of institutes and in the boards of various ministries, this does not rid it of the defects of a one-sided bureaucratic approach.

There is a great deal of testimony by scientists and engineers about how, in attempting to explain the essence of some matter to other people, even in ordinary, everyday terms, they found that many long-established, iron-clad ideas turned out to be shaky and questionable. When publicizing a professional, mature project, the authors cannot expect readers or television viewers to deluge them with fresh, brilliant ideas, although such situations have occurred. But when they know that their works and their names will inevitably be made public, the authors themselves will recheck everything according to objective criteria and not to someone's personal opinions; such "extra pressure" will eliminate many mistakes even before a project becomes public.

Broad public knowledge would not only make up for the dearth of ideas and information so evident in ecology, but it could also establish a special prestige and ethical monitoring among colleagues, among people in one field.

Accurate information about environmental problems is more necessary now than perhaps any other social or scientific information. Eco-information is an SOS that must be sent in all directions at once because we don't know from what quarter help may come. Everything we know about local ecological crises in past historical epochs tells us that they have always ended badly for the people or peoples who caused them. The current crisis is an incomparably more complex situation without parallel in history. Who would be so bold as to claim that he and his friends and acquaintances can find the way out of this dead end? That they and only they should be given control over all the ideas, all the information needed for research? Who would guarantee that the most valuable ideas for society might not be in the mind of some old man or boy who could neither back them up for lack of information nor publicize them because he is not "competent"?

What Central Committee, what Academy of Sciences can claim it has an exhaustive command of knowledge about problems that concern the fate of the world?

The likelihood that we will find a way out of the ecological impasse is not very great, but it will be precisely nil if the situation remains as it is——if the search for a way out of the ecological dead end remains in the hands of only a few "specially competent persons" rather than becoming the concern of our entire society.

By not giving people the opportunity to comprehend the true dimensions of the impending ecological peril, our leaders deprive them of the opportunity to mobilize all their forces, to win or lose, but to lose courageously, like a warrior who has spent everything possible for frail human nature. We have the right to win or lose ourselves and not turn things over to the "sages" who, having lost Azov, the Aral, the Caspian, and millions of square kilometers of land, continue to live in the lap of luxury and do not even deem it necessary to tell us about their failures.

If people don't perceive the dimensions of the real threat, they will not adopt the self-restraint needed for serious ecological action. And there can be but one outcome: after ecological disasters have hit, someone will have to do the restraining for them, by force, with all the ensuing consequences.

Hence to create the illusion that existing economic and ideological means are sufficient to deal with the problems of ecological disaster, or that the current course of the economy can steer the country away from the reefs and shoals toward which other countries are drifting——that is the gravest sin of Soviet propaganda. A sin unforgivable in its conciousness and premeditation.

It is turning the country into a kind of parody of the ill-famed *Titanic*. The fires had long spread into the various reaches of its hold, and the captain realized that they could be put out only by "all hands." Yet for the captain the honor of his uniform stood above everything in the world, and he would never in his life admit his own mistakes and stupidity. And even now he does not interrupt the meal in the crew's cabin; he holds his pose and orders water taken to the hold in tea cups——"in an emergency in teapots. . . ."

# 9 A Country in Reserve

The book Barbara Ward and Rene Dubos wrote especially for the Stockholm Conference of the United Nations on environmental conservation was entitled *Only One Earth*. "We cannot allow experiments to ascertain the maximum level of pollution life on earth can tolerate because we do not have a planet in reserve." This was the leitmotif of the Western ecologists' arguments.

In this respect the Soviet Union differs from every other country in the world: we have a country in reserve, a second USSR, as it were. Almost all the land we have in mind when we say "Siberia and the Far North" is still unpopulated, or more precisely, its population is eight to nine million people, which is 3.5 percent of the entire population of the country. Their territory, that is, Siberia (excluding the long-exploited southern regions, along the coast, around the Amur River, and Sakhalin) and the Far North, amounts to eleven million square kilometers, *almost half of the USSR*.

Siberia and the North include boundless plains, remote taiga, mountain ranges, and gigantic rivers and lakes. Here are found all our country's fabulous natural riches, about which every Soviet citizen hears from childhood onward. Much of this is true. Siberia is a unique chance for the Soviet system, a land where new relationships with nature could be built without repeating the gross errors of the past.

In 1917 the Soviet government obtained Siberia and the Far North in almost the same condition in which they were created by God, with the exception of the fur-bearing animals (the sable in particular) and gold. Hence the experiment in exploiting Siberia was a pure experiment, a kind of test for the socialist mode of development.

Now, however, there is a more important question: what is the state of nature in Siberia and the North today? Could this second country in reserve alleviate the ecological crisis that is intensifying in the European part of the country and in Central Asia? What can these lands provide now, when the need for them has become so serious and so urgent?

Even a cursory knowledge of nature in Siberia and the North[1] suggests that the permafrost and the severe climate make the development of natural resources there very difficult. There are strict limits on exploitation.

Even all the technological achievements in modern building, for example, the erection of large buildings on permafrost, give us no reason to believe that this problem has actually been solved. Hundreds of houses are abandoned each year in northern settlements because they collapse, their foundations settle, and cracks and breaks appear. Sometimes in old cemeteries bodies buried in coffins, as is the settlers' custom, are pushed by frost to the surface, where they thaw. These grisly incidents have become a grim symbol of the fact that the North will not tolerate the life style of the "newcomers" and their ever increasing pressure on it.

Only twenty years ago the frost absorbed, and in places even regurgitated, the infamous "road of the dead," built on Stalin's orders from Salekhard eastward for thousands of kilometers. Highways are still a problem, especially in the tundra. After a bit of traffic the track turns into impassible mud, and the road shifts to the left or right. Again and again. In the summer it is impossible to reach certain tundra settlements from any direction——everything is rutted and swampy tracks.

The tracks of all-terrain vehicles have been visible on the mossy surfaces of the tundra for four or five years. The gullies, often starting at the highway, grow at a rate of fifteen meters each summer. V. V. Kriuchkov, an expert on the North, entitled his book *The Delicate Subarctic*. He shows that all northern communities are examples of organisms' equilibrium at the brink of survival. Almost any disturbance by man destroys the fragile balance. Such gross disruptions as cutting trees in sparse forests and in the forest tundra have been catastrophic for the land. Around the "road of the dead" sand dunes, stagnant lakes, and buckles have formed in arid forest tundra areas just because all the trees were felled for 300 to 400 meters on both sides of the railroad line.

In Alaska rail-layers on pneumatic tires are used so as not to harm the mossy cover of the tundra, which preserves the frost. In Canada the whole of forest technology works without destroying the soil; and after the machines go, seeds can take root in their ruts. In our country forest technology is enemy No. 1 of the taiga undergrowth and the shallow taiga soils. Development of an ecological forest technology is planned for 1980-85. Only development . . .

The myth of the unspoiled expanses of our taiga and tundra spreads more swiftly than any other. Dozens of "Belgiums" and "Switzerlands" and hundreds of "Luxembourgs" turn out to be a fiction, since their nature is far less resistant to the impact of man than is nature in the actual Switzerland. After the geologists and oil and gas prospectors have passed through, the tundra or forest tundra in Taimyr and Yamal is "spoiled" far more than the nature around Moscow has been in a hundred years of exploitation.

The forests recede for kilometers from northern settlements not because of fellings but solely from the effect of hydrogen sulfide. The nomad camps of the Nentsy, the Chukchi, or the Eskimo were never especially agreeable places to the European eye and sense of smell. However, it is difficult to find a more chaotic and sorry sight than the streets and surroundings of modern cities and villages. For many kilometers around any village there is neither a tree nor even a bit of natural landscape —only littered, swampy wasteland where heaps of ash, slag, bottles, other rubbish, and the hulks of cars and trucks "abound." Nine or ten months of the year this littered wasteland is covered by snow, but for two or three months in the summer the sun shines on it round the clock, and it is almost the only scenery the inhabitants of the North see from the windows of their houses.

Ten times more fuel per capita is burned in modern housing in Siberia than was burned in the tents and tepees of the natives. This has gravely affected the air in the settlements. Ten months of smoky atmosphere, filthy snow, and dirty melt water kill all the moss and lichen in the surrounding area, and the bilberry ceases to bear fruit. Deprived of its covering of moss and lichen, the permafrost quickly turns into swamp. Atmospheric pollution in Siberia and the North in the winter (which is low compared to the central zone), combined with cold air, has a worse effect on the lungs of people than pollution in the southern regions. Moreover, in the North pollution swiftly reduces the ultraviolet light in the sun's rays since they must penetrate a much thicker layer of the atmosphere (due to the sun's low position). The number of days with fog in industrial Norilsk is twice as high as in Dudinka, located not too far away.

V. V. Kriuchkov asserts that the forests in the North are receding southward and shrinking rapidly, not from global changes in climate but from man's destruction of lichen and moss and the cooling of the soil that ensues, as well as from the mass felling and forest fires. The destruction of forests causes a perceptible drop in temperature and rise in winds, not vice-versa.

In the northern part of Siberia fires cause much more damage than in the south. According to statistics, nowhere does the forest burn more frequently thanks to people's carelessness than here. An unextinguished match, a cigarette butt, or sparks from an all-terrain vehicle ignite the dry moss, which burns like powder. Yet vehicles have still not been equipped with even the most rudimentary spark arresters.

In northern Yakutia alone more than 80,000 square kilometers (in journalese, two Switzerlands) have burned or been cut in the last three decades. Moreover, the woods destroyed in forest tundra and thin forest will never regenerate. Under present climatic conditions trees draw excess moisture from the soil, and with the trees gone the soil quickly turns to swamp.

Forests have always been cleared for meadows and pastures for domestic cattle. However, in the northern regions of Yakutia, and elsewhere, this is not appropriate over vast expanses. But present methods of economic management have a very suspicious attitude toward "scraps"; they want scale. And when large parcels are cleared of trees and brush, it turns out that their soils freeze much deeper than do small areas covered with brush; the frost rises to the surface in a few years, and the meadow——or plowland or garden——loses all value.

In Siberia hothouses require tremendous quantities of fuel. Yet so convenient and ecologically clean a source of energy for heat and light as wind-driven power plants are used practically nowhere. Hundreds of tons of coal are burned in the northern regions to produce, of all things, cold. Cold storage chambers in the permafrost, which would provide cheap, ideally steady cooling, are barely used by northern meat and fish combines.

The permafrost and low temperatures make problems of treatment almost insoluble in Siberia. Ordinary sewage does not seep into the soil and is not filtered, as in the south. Decomposition of wastes is twenty to thirty times slower. In the spring all the garbage is carried away in the rivers; and while an ordinary river cleans itself of permissible doses of organic matter within 200 to 300 kilometers, in the North even 1,500 kilometers are too few to do the job.[2]

Rivers large and small in Siberia and the North are being mercilessly mutilated by gold dredges. Picturesque and fertile valleys are being turned into dumps of gravel and shingle, and for hundreds of kilometers along their course the water is white or brown with roiled sand and silt. Even the simplest species of fish cannot survive in such water. Gold miners work not only along the river beds. The steep banks, which they have eroded, have become the source of slippages and slides that clog streams and rivulets. All gold-mining enterprises discharge unfiltered wastes.[3] The lack of ceremony of the gold miners is easily explained: gold is a "strategic product." A few years ago, at a meeting of the Magadan Regional Committee of the CPSU, one of the country's high-ranking officials asked executives in the gold industry what they would need to be able to immediately speed deliveries of gold beyond the plan. Among the "bottlenecks" the latter named the requirements of the water and land conservation inspectorates. By a personal order the high-ranking official suspended all the environmental protection laws in those areas where gold was mined.

During the '30s, '40s, and even the '50s, environmental protection problems did not even exist in Siberia and the North. Even the term "protection" was understood by everyone only as the military guard, armed to the teeth, in the concentration camps.

Today conferences are held in Siberia, and articles and books are published on the problems of environmental protection and the conservation of natural resources. But is limited freedom of investigation and discussion sufficient to prevent the grossest mistakes from being repeated? Has the exploitation of Siberian forests and useful minerals become ecologically more sensible?

On the one hand, along the path of the Baikal-Amur Mainline (BAM) can be found more examples of intelligent, sensitive treatment of the forest and the landscape as a whole than on any other building site of former times. Yet the scale of the destruction of nature around the railway exceeds anything previously known.

Academician Baroian, one of the leaders of Soviet microbiology, in an article on the problems of BAM health and ecology, noted quite pointedly that "the majority of catastrophic smogs in capitalist countries occur where there is little wind and where pollution is difficult to disperse." Behind this Aesopian statement stands the fact that over the Yakutsk tract (and there "you can gallop for three years and never run across capitalism") and in Tynda heavy "smog" frequently descends in the winter. Since in the winter there is no wind, the threat of smog is obvious for the entire western section of the BAM.

In the opinion of specialists, production of automobile and tractor motors adapted to the severe northern winter would help more than anything else to beat the smog. There is nothing strange in this: since it is impossible to start their motors in the mornings, the drivers frequently let the vehicles run all night in neutral, and, of course, air pollution increases.

"A warm toilet" was a saying in the parlance of satirists and born jokesters in the '50s and '60s, a handy phrase whenever talk turned to exploitation of Siberia and the North. They reduced the whole wretched life of the "colonizers" in the North to the "warm toilet left in Moscow." Now along the BAM and elsewhere, houses are built with all the conveniences, but this has given rise to another difficulty—where to empty the sewage systems if in the winter the rivers freeze to the bottom and nothing decomposes in the soil?

What to do with the 500 kilograms of garbage accumulated per capita each year on the BAM? The spread of synthetics and other new materials has created a situation in which new settlements become littered many times faster than did old ones, despite all the conveniences. In BAM settlements there are no plans to do anything but burn the rubbish, but that will only augment the menace of smog. Academician Baroian acknowledges that neither scientists nor engineers have yet found ecological methods for eliminating wastes in the North.

The ecological problems of the BAM mount with each passing day. Dozens of small rivers are turned into gullies filled with muddy water after builders extract their gravel for railroad embankments. As a result of this and of oil pollution, fish have almost disappeared from rivers in settled regions. There is no use talking about restricting the hunting season; for many kilometers around populated centers both birds and animals are overhunted, and berry bushes and nut trees—a major source of food for animals—no longer bear fruit. The ecological equilibrium has been disrupted, and the "green desert" will not remain green very long without animals, even if it is not cut down.

Mountain ranges large and small occupy a large part of the

BAM region; but after clearing, the mountain forests hardly ever regenerate. The thin soil layer is easily eroded from the slopes after felling; the permafrost reaches the surface, and trees can hardly take root. Studies by botanists and forestry experts in Siberia have shown that barely 20 percent of all cleared forests have been restored throughout the whole northeast of Siberia.[4]

Of all the territories in Siberia and the North, nature in the Northeast, which will also be developed by the BAM, is the most unstable and vulnerable. These are not mere words. The famous ecologist Eugene Odum calculated the relationship between untouched and exploited areas for certain belts in the United States. In the south, according to Odum, 40 percent of the land can be taken up by cities, roads, airports, and cultivated lands, while 60 percent should remain as forests, swamps, plains, and other natural landscapes open for recreation, moderate hunting, fishing, and selective logging. Otherwise the ecological balance there will be irreversibly disrupted. According to calculations by Soviet ecologists, this relationship should not be more than 20 percent and 80 percent for Siberia and the North, while for the mountain territories and the Far North it should even be 10 percent and 90 percent.

The biological output per hectare of tundra, forest tundra, and northern taiga is dozens of times less than in central zones. This factor largely determines the potential for exploiting resources and the chances for providing the population there a normal life; no technology can increase the biological output to any major extent.[5]

What specifically are the burdens the Northeast and other regions of the "second USSR" can tolerate? How should they be distributed?

Various studies on the problems of the BAM are being carried out in dozens of institutions, including at the Institute of the Geography of Siberia and the Far East at Irkutsk. The Irkutsk researchers harbor no illusions regarding the adoption of their ecological recommendations.

"Our task is to elucidate the processes taking place——soil, hydrological, and topographical——as reliably as we can and to provide sound recommendations for any case," said one of the officials of the Institute of Geography. "But you probably know as well as I what we can really expect. First, the fish and the animals disappear, then come the forest fires and insects, blockages in the rivers, fellings, and finally, slides, mud torrents, floods, and so forth."

Aside from general discussions on the relationship between actively exploitable lands and untouched lands (10 percent and 90 percent), the recommendations of the scientists contain too much that is inapplicable for present methods of developing Siberia and the North. Such development entails a careful, personal approach to each exploitable area; the decentralization of many industries, which would considerably increase their cost; a minimal number of people, especially in the Far North. But this approach does not square with the goal of cheap production of our resources for ourselves and for sale abroad, which is the current rationale for developing Siberia and the North; so the recommendations of "science" will remain recommendations. Nothing forbids their implementation, but they are intentions, not *a plan*.

In some way or other almost all recommendations stress the need for changes not only in the technological but also in the social and psychological aspects of development. And while everything is clear with technology, at least in theory, the situation is worse with regard to psychological and social changes. It is not clear even what changes should take place to make man's relations with nature in Siberia and the North more harmonious. It is only clear what changes *must not take place*. They must not be the ones going on now.

The "second USSR," our "country in reserve," is a unique land where almost the entire population is present on assignment. Even Russians and Ukrainians born and raised there regard themselves as transients. Nine out of ten are looking for ways to earn a bit more and get back to "civilization" a bit sooner. Many of them are not released because of convictions or other crimes and delinquencies; but artificially making them northerners does not give them a feeling for the North as their homeland, a sense of involvement in the fate of this land. To work sensibly, with verve, taking into account all the complex local natural factors—most people do not want to do this, indeed cannot. (Perhaps the situation is no better elsewhere, but in the North carelessness costs nature far more.)

It is difficult, however, to blame the negligence of the settlers for everything. Figures tell us that 30 percent of those who have lived in the North for three or four years return as invalids, that is, with a medically certified disability classification.

All colonization has begun with the colonization of the land, with farming colonies. And the fate of the newcomers has depended on how they have been able to adapt to the land. The modern era of development of Siberia and the North has not made the settlers into a group of people vitally interested in sensible, nonpredatory use of the new lands. Development today is urban, industrial colonization, a foreign body both for nature and the native peoples of Siberia and the North.

A journalist visiting Taimyr told this story. At a boarding school for Nentsy, Dolgan, and Nganasan children in Dudinka, he asked the children how they spent the holidays in the tundra. While most of the children muttered by rote that they helped their native collective farm and the like, one little girl told him quietly:

> "I saw the shaman. He came to us when we were pasturing our deer. He prayed."
> "What did he pray for? Did he ask God for good weather?"
> "No, he asked for the Russians to go away."

The contradictions between the civilizations of the "big time" and the "local backwater" begin with basics, with psychology, with attitudes toward the land. For the "white man" arriving with the best intentions, the North is a white desert, regardless of what grows there or does not; it is a void that must be filled with the meaning and light of the European industrial way of life. In sum, it gets filled with garbage. But it all begins with psychology.

Here is how a journalist quite convinced of the correctness and virtue of "progress" describes the tundra.

> I looked into the map illuminator. Below us was the unpeopled and lifeless tundra. Across the barren earth, dotted with swamps, was sparse, frail, and fragile lichen—and emptiness: neither beast nor bird nor even smoke on the horizon. A sense of dead silence and tangible primitiveness. As if we were no longer on the earth but on another, lifeless planet that had not yet been touched by the breath of life.[6]

(Another time, another area of Siberia, another style, but otherwise it has a great deal in common with Zazubrin's 1926 iron and concrete calls to eradicate the whole of Siberia as it had been.)

For a Chukchi or a Nenets "the dead, lifeless tundra" is just as vital a world as France or Greece is for a European, or the Sahara is for a Bedouin. The local deer herder sees thousands of nuances of life inaccessible to the newcomer. He finds his flocks from their reflection on low-lying clouds dozens of kilometers away; the language of the northern people has not just one word for "snow"——there are dozens of words for every possible kind of snow: blizzard, drift, falling, dry, moist . . .

When the journalist asked the children at the boarding school whether they liked it in the Crimea, in Artek, where they went for the summer, they nodded their heads, yes, they liked it.

"And do you want to go again?"

"No. It's nicer in the tundra."

Until recently the world of the tundra was for its people a special world, with spirits reincarnated in rocks, in the underground warm tundra, with its myths, embodying truths of human existence no less profound than the mythologies of other peoples.

Simchenko, an expert on the ethnography of the North, writes that at an international conference he was asked whether our minor northern peoples were becoming extinct?

"No," answered Simchenko. "On the contrary, their numbers are growing, and growing well."[7]

And he presented statistical data.

All well and good. There is no reason to reproach Simchenko. Except that statistics are, as we know, a third form of lie.

Simchenko knows perfectly well what the old shaman had in mind, and what Simchenko's colleagues at the Institute of Ethnography of the Academy of Sciences write in their secret reports: that as they grow in numbers, almost all the peoples of the North degenerate as nations.[8]

The Nentsy, Dolgan, or Chukchi family now has seven or eight children. But local customs and conditions of life are such that five or six of them are usually by different "white" fathers. As the specialists say, the genetic pool of the minor peoples is not being preserved.

The children, raised from the first grade onward in boarding schools, retain few of the cultural attributes of their nation. The children know both Russian and their own language poorly; they forget the work habits of their fathers and grandfathers, while they absorb all the worst aspects of modern urban civilization. Ethnographers talk about the rapid disintegration of nations——soon ethnography will have nothing to study. Many of the northerners can no longer even be ascribed any nationality as far as way of life and physical and psychological characteristics are concerned. Unless it is the "Russian alcoholic civilization," since drunkenness begins here at the age of thirteen or fourteen.

The civilization of recent decades has saved many of the northern peoples from the degeneration caused by their contact with nineteenth-century civilization. Their physical condition has improved: now no one dies of hunger in the tundra; but the traditional way of life and economy have been undermined.

In the past their way of life was intimately bound up with the course of natural phenomena and totally depended on variations in the climate and animal population. Even if total ecological balance between environment and man here was doubtful, the economy was stable. During cold periods the number of deer increased sharply, and the tribes migrated into the tundra. Ten to fifteen years later it warmed up, epizootics decimated the deer, and the tribes returned to the seashore to hunt for marine animals. They preserved their tools and their habits of flexible adaptation to local conditions: shifting from a nomadic to a settled life and back again.

Today's methods of deer raising and fishing on collective farms and state farms, the entire planned economy, simply pay no attention to the dynamics of natural conditions, to cool snaps, heat waves . . . The dynamics of the plan are always the same, whether in the black-earth belt or in the North: year in and year out, constant growth in output. Deer epizootics in warm years, fluctuations in the number of marine animals—in recent years hunting experts and zoologists have begun to study them, but their recommendations have had negligible influence on running these businesses. As before, plans are fulfilled only in favorable years, and throughout the entire North profitable enterprises have been but the few isolated exceptions. The others survive on subsidies.

The permanent settlements in the North are suited only to teaching children in schools and to providing medical and cultural facilities for the population. To say nothing of the fact that they exert enormous pressure on the countryside: it is impossible to farm in them, there is nothing for people to do. Thirty or forty shepherds tend their deer, 200 or 300 members of the collective farm in the village administer and provide one another with services: the same thing takes place in the shore settlements and in the administrative centers, a kind of Provident Haven.

New occupations dreamed up in Vladivostok or Moscow

for the population of the North are usually striking in their senselessness.

One sorry tale was the breeding of polar foxes on farms. Sorry because to feed the voracious foxes whales were killed, including, of course, very rare species, females, and the young. Harpooners easily distinguish authorized from prohibited species by their spout; but they are always paid for the number of carcasses, and there has never been a case in which a harpooner was punished for a mistake. They *are* punished for nonfulfillment of the plan.

The killed whales were butchered on the shore, and long strips of meat and blubber were taken to the farms on tractors. If after eating the whales the foxes did not die from an epizootic within the next month, then death took them the following year. The average mortality for foxes reached 90 percent. The cost of one fox fur is 400 to 500 rubles. It was sold to the government for 49 rubles. The plan for foxes was the top priority for the collective farms. Far from the coast dogs were shot in the settlements and deer were butchered for food for the foxes.

The fox farms have been quietly closing in recent years, but intensive enlargement of the settlements has begun. The last walruses have left the once teeming breeding grounds around Shmidt Cape and Ryrkapii Village because of the concentration of population, the accumulation of noisy machinery, and smoke pollution. In the same area, on Chukotka, the pasture land is rapidly deteriorating from the excessive grazing of deer. Today the lichens, the main fodder for deer, cover only 1 to 3 percent of the land area, yet only eighty years ago Captain Billings described huge white expanses—white with lichens—dominating the landscape.

There are people who have experienced the tragic metamorphosis of the northern peoples deeply and seriously. Through their tremendous efforts, at the end of the fifties an experimental forestry collective farm was organized in the Evenki taiga. The ethnographers intended for the local inhabitants to carry on with their traditional way of life, raising deer and hunting on a specified territory without the interference of the "planned economy" and modern industries.

"Ten years later I returned there," one of the organizers of the experimental forestry farm told us, "and what I saw was much worse than before our arrangements. Both the people and nature. It was horrible."

"Well, then, did you do something?" one of his audience asked.

"I cried," said the scientist, a man who had been through the war and knew Siberia and the North not just from rosy tourist slides.

If only the improbable were to happen, if only God would hear the prayers of the old shaman and grant them—and the Russians would go away. Would the economy of the North then develop along the lines of its own traditions? Would its relations with nature then be harmonious?

Studies by ethnographers have shown that even during the period of traditional primitive economy, such harmony did not exist. It is nice to think that tribes living by hunting, fishing, and primitive agriculture did not go so far as to totally deplete their only resource and did not seriously upset the ecological balance. Studies by ethnographers on the life of the Chukchi and the Eskimo at the end of the last and during the first third of the present century paint a different picture.

There were quite a number of prohibitions on killing animals: does and the young. Nonetheless the Chukchi killed whales, walruses, and beluga whales beyond their needs, beyond the point of security for future herds.

The northerners killed as many wild deer as they could, and they stockpiled helpless birds during moult in such numbers that they spoiled and were not fit even to feed dogs.[9]

This was not done out of rapaciousness in our sense of the word. Fluctuations in the climate and in the number of animals in the North are such that if man did not learn to use every chance to get food, he would simply not survive there. The appearance of firearms introduced essentially nothing new. Studies show that the rituals that existed, for example, the obligatory offering of a deer's eyes to the earth ("otherwise the deer will go away"), the invocations and prayers of the shamans, gave the appearance that man lived in conformity with all the laws of savage nature and remained flesh of its flesh. Rituals created a psychological harmony; however, a real ecological balance, a balance in the exchange of matter and energy between man and other communities of animals and plants could not be ensured by rituals. Rather, they supported and legitimated man's constant impulses toward "expanded reproduction," clothing aggression and the destruction of natural equilibrium in the guise of total submission to the higher forces of nature.

Some taiga peoples, for example, the western Siberian Selkups, had real natural taboos, sacred forest altar-caches for each tribe, and families venerated the taiga around them for dozens of kilometers. In these areas not only hunting but gathering mushrooms and nuts and felling trees for camp fires were forbidden. But it must be said that the Selkups' economic setup has not been subjected to so thorough an analysis as has that of Chukotka.

It is not impossible that even the sacred caches and preserves were inadequate, and perhaps even the celebrated Dersu Uzala was a member of a tribe that lived precisely by the law of psychological unity with surrounding nature. Arsenev and other Europeans were unable to detect any indications of natural greediness, since Dersu and his fellow tribesmen were few in number, and their actions destroyed natural ecosystems much more slowly than does our way of life.

The rates at which northerners' actions degraded nature in the past and in the current century are, of course, not comparable. Yet the Chukotka Eskimo always tried to kill young whales rather than adults for the pot, since their meat was tastier. So it had been before, when whales were plentiful, and so it is now; and neither traditional taboos nor the explanations and the prohibitions of new authorities have been able to protect whales from extinction.

Other studies, this time by archeologists, bear out the view that harmony between man and nature is some sort of ideal state that has existed in reality only by chance. Analysis of the bones of animals found in Neolithic camps shows a preponderance of remains of young mammoths and not mature individuals. The young were killed because their meat was much more tender, tastier, although one adult mammoth provided as much meat and nutrition as many young. Whether Neolithic man was aware that by interfering with the mammoths' reproduction he was doing harm to himself no one can say, but specialists have calculated that it was the "gourmandizing" inclinations of our remote ancestors that were responsible for these huge animals' disappearance from the face of the earth.

Of course, we are not talking about the roots of the contradictions between man and the animal and plant world in which he lives in order to dissipate the problems of the exploitation of Siberia and the North in historical perspective. Whatever the historical and biological precedents, the clean pages of the huge "second USSR" were smeared not by the natives but by our own civilization, and mainly in the last fifty years.

Objective geographic, climatic, and other conditions of Siberia and the North have dictated other methods for exploiting the land than those used in central latitudes. The abundance of biological resources there is illusory, as Shtilmark, the Siberian expert, writes: "Fish catches seem so huge there only to those who drop their nets for the first time. The second time the catch is much smaller, and the third time the net is almost empty."[10] It will take tens, even hundreds of years to restore the fish, the animals, or the cedar crop. This is provided that resources are not exhausted and natural conditions do not change for the worse.

The total lack of roads and the remoteness of industrial bases have also dictated other methods of exploitation. Taking into account both natural and economic factors, the most rational is the "tour-of-duty" method for exploiting resources. Small settlements to which people are brought specifically to work when everything needed for construction has been delivered would be the best solution from an ecological and economic point of view. Today in the BAM zone and practically throughout the entire North, normal work goes on for half a year and sometimes for only three or four months a year. The rest of the time material and equipment are brought in and repairs are made.

Economists take into account only the losses from the average wage needed to keep a worker the year round. The ecological damage inflicted on the surrounding taiga and rivers by such inappropriately overgrown permanent settlements is actually much greater.

But the development of Tiumen oil and forests, copper, and coal in the BAM zone is a special kind of salvage operation; it is a crutch for the economy's disintegrating plan system. It is a crutch paid for by the export of natural resources. Given such an approach, in which everything is determined by "strategic" goals—keeping the system of running the country and the economy unchanged in its earlier form and reinforcing the military might of the country in the East (also by earlier methods)—the only place left for ecology is on the pages of newspapers. The fact that most of the exploited resources given such an approach are resources that can be used only one time does not change anything. The net is tossed the first time, the second time, but what then? Let come what may.

In this chapter we have not touched on any of the concrete examples of the devastation of nature in West Siberia by today's rapid methods of extracting oil and gas. Two facts, however, are worth mentioning: the decomposition of oil which has gotten into water depends primarily on temperature, which determines the growth of bacteria that break it down (at low temperatures oil slicks float for years in the northern seas without diminishing); second, West Siberia, as we know, is a region saturated with water, where there are more marshes and lakes than solid ground. Hence the thousands of oil wells where environmental protection does not rank second or even tenth on the agenda, the thousands of oil wells where water is pumped out of oil strata and poured into rivers and lakes are a threat, without exaggeration, to all nature in West Siberia. And this threat is not merely for the five or six years when resources are being exploited but for tens and hundreds of years, since the gathering and recovery of oil from Siberian marshes and rivers is a task even less realistic than cleaning up polluted Baikal.

We have not spoken here about the threat that hangs over nature in all the BAM regions, which extend, as the economists say, over 3.5 million square kilometers (all of Western Europe); we have said nothing about the Southern Yakutsk Industrial Complex, about the Magadan and Chukotka polymetal belt and the diamond belt of Yakutia, about the Undokan copper region, about the Pevek mines, where the destruction of forests and the pollution of rivers and the air are growing literally with each passing day. We have not mentioned the Ust-Ilimsk paper and pulp combine, which after start-up will each year denude enough taiga land to equal two or three Luxembourgs; nor have we described the mountains of rotting red fish in the estuaries of the Amur and other rivers flowing into the Okhotsk Sea (and now during the fish runs more fish are caught than the fish factories can handle, since this is what the *plan* impels the fishermen to do!). We have not talked about many other things.

But just a list of these areas reminds us that untouched Siberia is an illusion, that industry is devouring the "green, fragile bosom of Siberia" from all sides, like sulfuric acid, and has already reached its radiant orb——Baikal. It reminds us that current methods for exploiting Siberia are ways to destroy it. As before, virtually no stratum of indigenous northerners has been created; and the enthusiastic first BAM settlers, having worked their three years and earned their promised Zhiguli cars, try to get away however they can. As before, temporary and seasonal labor works there. Such methods of exploitation are unsatisfactory from both the social point of view (they do not provide a normal, healthy life for the local population, and their expansion is at the expense of the newcomers) and the economic (they prove too costly). Ecologically, Siberia may very soon be transformed from "an inexhaustible source of resources" into a disaster area. Within fifteen to twenty years our "country in reserve" may be a frozen wasteland, and restoring it to life will be harder than revitalizing the burning deserts of Central Asia.

The answer to the questions we posed at the beginning of the chapter might go as follows: Siberia and the North have considerable natural resources, but at present prompt efforts are necessary *to prevent the "second USSR" from being destroyed before the first one.*

Modern science cannot cope with its main task in society: to ensure the survival of this society. Soviet ecology cannot even cope with part of this task. It does not even have the courage to warn us about the impending danger.

Nor can Soviet philosophy or Soviet journalism cope with it. Although some semifictional works, such as *King Fish* by V. Astafiev or *Farewell to Mother* by V. Rasputin, contain more tragic truth about the destruction of nature than do strictly scientific works.

But neither documentary books with the gloomiest statistics nor the most brilliant metaphors and descriptions of the human spirit experiencing the devastation of its native climes are in themselves likely to change anything.

Only the joint efforts of that "legion of scientists and writers of whatever sort," which, as Pushkin wrote, bears true enlightenment and culture despite curses and attacks from all sides, can get public awareness on the march. But where is that legion? Where is it in all the field from Kulikovo to Baikal?

# 10 Taking Stock: (Or: Who Will Pay for the Tragedy?)

*"The doctor and the physician, seeing that their tidings did not please Tsar Boris, did not want to treat the Danish prince. . . . So Godunov did away with the prince."*
*Chronicle of the Russian Ruin* (end of sixteenth century, Boris Godunov's era)

Simultaneously with the "pay for pollution" system at the Central Economic-Mathematical Institute, another project on the environment was under way. K. Gofman, doctor of economic sciences, had set up a scale with which one could graphically evaluate the state of the environment. In the United States there are several such rating systems, one of which is based on a simple hundred-point principle. In 1972, according to it, the index for the state of the environment in the United States was 53 points while in 1973 it was 52.

Gofman based his scale on man's needs for basic natural resources (100 percent) and the degree to which they are met. A similar rating of industrial goods and foodstuffs shows that the needs of the Soviet citizen are being met 60 to 70 percent. But on Gofman's scale we satisfy only 5 to 10 percent of needs with natural resources!

If you want to live in a city with clean air but actually have a chance to live where the atmosphere contains 20 MPCs of carbon monoxide and other gases, that is, air twenty times worse than the norm, your needs are met 5 percent. If you would like to relax near a clean and blue sea, and in fact you can only choose between Yalta, Sukhumi, Tuapse, and Odessa, where oil and phenol pollution is at least 10 MPCs, you are satisfied 10 percent.

The scale evoked a number of accusations of idealism. Let

us assume that some of them are valid. But even if Gofman's ratings are somewhat toned down, the state of the environment in the USSR still provokes extreme concern for our lives.

That clean air has become a rarity is a fact even our lungs recognize—it is obvious. That nature is being destroyed our own eyes tell us, the figures tell us. But how bad is the devastation of nature in our country? How does the burden of this destruction touch the ordinary citizen?

Apart from the Gofman scale, there is no other known system for assessing the general state of the environment. Even the forecasts *Nature 1980* and *Nature 1990* avoid giving absolute, if not relative, estimates of the destruction of our land, rivers, and lakes. They provide no overall statistics on this field of activity in our society. To get precise information on impoverished bodies of water, on mountains and forests turned into deserts and semideserts, one must have a special satellite. The effects of the devastation rarely strike the eye: miners and lumberjacks milk the mutilated land of its resources and then leave them with nothing for the traveler, let alone the tourist, to do. Entire collective farms have abandoned fields made worthless by erosion in the Trans-Volga area, in the North Caucasus, and in Georgia. Even biologists and ecologists see these "badlands" from afar, in passing. Who has seen with his own eyes more than a dozen such areas, more than a dozen garbage dumps? But there are more than 1,500 industrial and over 4,000 urban dumps in the country.

Nonetheless one can get a reliable idea of what is taking place if one analyzes a large number of official publications, books, and articles.

The entire country, the entire area of the planet now colored red on the globe, covers 22 million square kilometers, as we know from our schoolbooks. Water, perpetual ice and snow, barren crags—in a word, uninhabitable land—occupy about one third, so that of the 22 million, 14 to 15 million square kilometers remain for us. That is the whole "pie." Now let's figure out who gets what slice.

In 1977:

—175,000 to 220,000 square kilometers (17.5-22.0 million hectares) are covered by lands mutilated and made worthless by mining and peat works;

—50,000 square kilometers (5 million hectares) go to dumps, tailings, slag, and sludge heaps from industrial enterprises, as well as municipal dumps;

—120,000 square kilometers (12 million hectares) are buried under the waters of large reservoirs;

—500,000 to 550,000 square kilometers (50-55 million hectares) are forest barrens and swamps left from logging and fires, which will not support even weeds;

—630,000 square kilometers (63 million hectares) are severely eroded, salinated land (plowland and pastures and meadows), ravines, and sand dunes in place of former fields.[1]

The total: 1.45 million square kilometers of now sterile land, industrial wasteland or semiwasteland.

This represents about 10 percent of the entire habitable territory of the USSR. And this tenth of our "pie," which we have devoured in little bites, was the most "succulent and tasty." The most suitable for use and, in many cases, the most fertile. We have picked the cherry from the cupcake. Hence we are parcelling out the second, third, and fourth shares as fast as possible. Especially since there are so many more of us, and our needs are growing at a very rapid pace.

If bourgeois Western Europe had treated its environment as we have, all the inhabitants of England, France, Italy, West Germany, Switzerland, and the Benelux countries would long ago have found themselves in a sterile desert. Their population is equal to ours—240-250 million—but their total land area is approximately one tenth of ours—1.4 million square kilometers.

I. Laptev, one of the ideologues of our country's ecological policy and a functionary for the Central Committee of the CPSU, stated in one of his articles that a society's attitudes toward nature bear the mark of all the relations and attitudes that have evolved within the society.[2] On this point we must agree with him.

"The depraved relations" that have evolved in our society do serious harm to our environment. The relationships between defects in the economic system and ecology are much more extensive than might appear at first glance.

They are:

—the chronic shortage of meat in the country—and the low productivity of collective farm stock raising—as well as the barbaric extermination of whales in the world's oceans and the coastal waters of the Far East;

—the same shortage of meat—and the organized poaching of birds on wintering grounds in the Kyzyl-Agach Preserve. Poaching that incidentally is annihilating the little bustard, the flamingo, the red-breasted goose, the black partridge, and dozens of other species listed in the Red Book;

——the low productivity of collective farm stock raising—— and the sharp decline of all species of deer and elk in Siberia and the Far East;

——a situation in which the Ministry of Agriculture is the sole proprietor of all the country's farmlands, while the collective farm workers have become indifferent to the land——and hasty, ill-considered reclamation that is ruining a large portion of the land, forests, berrying, and hunting grounds;

——a situation in which a huge share of our cotton and paper pulp goes for the manufacture of powder and other explosives (vast stockpiles of armaments for ourselves and for export)——and the excessive exploitation of all cotton-growing land in Central Asia as well as overcutting of forests. One might say that the successes of African and Asian national liberation movements, fighting with Soviet weapons, have been paid for with the destruction of many square kilometers of Siberian taiga;

——the recurrent need to purchase wheat and new technology abroad——and the devastation of rivers and river valleys in Siberia thanks to gold mining at any price.

In turn, the degradation of the environment has an impact on economic development. The wheat harvest on fields exposed to factory smoke is reduced by 30 to 60 percent. The forest has ceased to grow over broad areas. The pollution of rivers has reduced the value of meadows and pasture lands in their valleys to nothing.

The "great watershed" of 1929, as well as other "turning points" of the thirties and forties, the great construction campaigns of the five-year plans and the virgin lands, and the immediate strategic interests of the military, which shaped the fate of Baikal, are all factors that have affected our attitudes toward nature.

If today all pollution of the environment were suddenly to stop magically, the pollutants accumulated over the past years would continue to effect several subsequent generations as much as they do us.

If again by magic all the wretched legacy of "poor, backward Russia," the Second World War, "Stalin's excesses," and the Hydrological Planning Service were to disappear, it would hardly reduce the plundering of nature. Not now nor for several more generations. The main reasons for the devastation of nature lie more in our present than in our past.

The phenomenal development of science is the greatest pride of modern times. Science has become a productive force, as we all know. What is probably less known is how much it produces in our society. The contribution of science to the annual growth of USSR national income is 4 percent.[3]

Whereas in the past delays in introducing scientific discoveries retarded only the technical progress of production, now a slow development and introduction of ecological equipment and technology directly affect the state of the environment. The inability of our economy to realize its scientific potential is just as much a cause of the degradation of nature as the poor productivity of collective farm agriculture.

The figure 4 percent will shake even the most optimistic faith in the power of modern science. It is powerful only under certain social conditions.

How to change this situation?

How to interest industry in replenishing natural resources?

How to rectify inefficiency in agriculture?

How to see that legal measures effectively safeguard nature?

Wherever one traces the thread of ecology, it always leads deep into the economic and social structure of society.

Studies by all leading scientists say the same thing: large-scale ecological problems cannot be resolved solely within the framework of ecology, solely within the framework of technology, or even within the framework of pure economics. They require simultaneous changes both in the economy and in the social and moral foundations of society.

We are approaching the issue of the possibility of reforms, of necessary changes that would, at least, slow the pace of the degradation, the impoverishment of nature and, ideally, would ensure the ecological well-being of our people in the future.

It goes without saying that the specific content of such reforms is an extremely complicated matter, a subject for the efforts of many government minds. We are speaking now only of the chances for such reforms. Do they exist? Who would venture such reforms and why?

The burden of ecological problems is shared far from equally by various groups and strata of the population. We all breathe roughly the same air and walk on the same earth; but with that, equality in our socialist society ends.

Sociological statistics say that about 5 to 6 percent of our population lives wholly at the expense of the state (this is not to be confused with social security), i.e., in practical terms, beyond the economic laws of society. Regardless of the achievements of our agriculture and industry, 12 to 15 million of the top party and government leadership and members of their families have access to the goods of the twentieth century. These include the best, the "cleanest" environment.

Another 8 to 9 percent of the population—top military and scientific circles, the elite of the official art world, and the "new bourgeoisie" (dealers in commercial goods)—have enough money to buy or acquire everything they want. This includes suburban houses in the lap of nature. The other 85 to 87 percent, the majority of the population living on wages, feel the direct effects of the "hitches" in production and supply. This majority lives in concrete cells in crowded houses indistinguishable from what our propaganda just fifteen years ago was calling "the jungles of capitalist cities." This majority willingly suffers from the noise, the smog of those cities where they can find better paid jobs, where they can find some products to buy, let alone worrying about the carcinogens, allergens, or substances causing chromosomal mutations present there.

More than 85 percent of the population has no way to get real information about pollution; and if they think at all about ecology, it is usually only after they have contracted some sort of lung cancer and have been granted sufficient recuperation time in a hospital bed.

But the avant-garde of the people, as some of the representatives of the ruling elite call themselves, perceives the acuity of ecological problems only from the figures in various documents. The green fences around their suburban houses effectively screen them from the effects of both the economic and ecological crises. Five to six percent of our society has access to natural products (to the extent that this is now possible at all), special drinking water, and special swimming pools with filtered sea water (without oil and phenol).

Hence for us everything will always be ecologically all right. In fenced wild forests there will be enough "wild boars" to hunt; in lakes screened by underwater nets there will be fish for anglers. And no matter how Baikal is degraded, they will try to keep a few bays in virgin splendor, with pines on the high banks and the purest water, "where you can see every stone on the bottom." For them, for their guests, and sometimes for journalists and TV reporters there will be a clean Baikal and its *omul* salmon.

The bourgeois slogan—"Everyone pollutes, both producers and consumers, so everyone must pay for pollution"—is appropriate only for capitalists, the ideologue I. Laptev tells us.[4] The affluent classes in the West hardly suffer seriously from the ecological crisis, although even Soviet authors acknowledge that their incomes have declined somewhat due to expenditures for environmental protection. But how much of a burden have our elite 5 to 6 percent, to which Laptev belongs, assumed? He and his colleagues direct the whole of the country's industry, but have they paid even a bit? On the other hand, of course, Marshal Batitskii can no longer shoot polar bears from his helicopter. This is certainly a tremendous deprivation we cannot appreciate.

But we can understand that given such a distribution of the burden of environmental pollution among various strata of society, the chances for changing the situation are not great.

Government experts and referees know quite well about the true extent of the degradation of nature and how this threatens the country's future. They know it from studies by the Club of Rome and from our own forecasts, such as *Nature 1980* and *Nature 1990*, although the latter intentionally tone down the expected consequences. Semiofficially, ecological policy-makers explicate the government's present position roughly as follows:

Of course the state of the environment leaves much to be desired. Of course we destroy a lot and do so pointlessly. But it is no secret that investments in ecology are generally irretrievable and that this too is a question of strategy. As long as we do not invest very much, we can spend more on boosting the economy and on other targets. The more we are forced to invest, the less is left for economic development. In terms of land mass and many resources, our situation is better; hence we should use this strategic advantage over the United States.

Not only coal, oil, and other minerals but also clean air, the soil, and water must now be counted among our natural and strategic resources. The vast expanses of unused lands, which could be used for dumping without spending millions to bury and eliminate wastes, are also a strategic reserve. The advantages of space were once acquired by the tsarist autocracy, but now they serve the triumph of the ideas of communism. We have more air into which we can spew the smoke of factories without

risking suffocation; we have plenty of Baikal water that is diffi-
cult to pollute permanently; hence we can wait and accumulate
funds while capitalism suffocates in its smoke——in both the
literal and metaphorical sense, in the fumes of inflation. Right?

What part of the country can still be sacrificed so that the
moneys saved on Baikal, the Sea of Azov, and on protecting the
soil and water can be spent on "strategic and ideological pow-
er"??? How many dozens of countries can be devastated so that
the last man in our civilization speaks Russian, and then just
Marxist phrases? . . .

One would like to think that no one argues so fanatically.

The USSR's advantages in natural resources are substantial;
our bough is actually thicker, but thicker does not always mean
stronger. It does not mean that we can whittle away at it longer
than the Americans or the West in general do theirs.

Estimates by economists say that ten years ago, when the
ecological clouds had only begun to thicken, our society could
compensate for each ruble of damage from pollution with fifty
kopecks spent on environmental protection measures. Today
compensation for each ruble of damages costs about 1.5 to 1.7
rubles. And after 1982-83 compensation for a ruble's damages
will cost 3 to 3.5 rubles.

These statistics, and others, sit on the desks of the respon-
sible leaders of the State Planning Committee and departments
of the Central Committee; but as long as the objectives of spread-
ing the USSR's political and ideological influence in the world
are the prime elements in government policy, our attitude to-
ward nature will not change. Among all the announced mea-
sures to protect the environment, there is one area where these
steps have a good effect: it is propaganda, the showcase. The
money invested in pilot-demonstration enterprises, in blustery
articles that laud every such enterprise at each stage——in plan-
ning, at the start of construction, the end of building, opening,
and so on——yields greater gains than all other protective mea-
sures. This money serves to placate society; it yields advantage
in the form of enraptured neophytes and proselytes in Third
World countries and in the West.

Our nature, our home is being destroyed by us. The roof
in our home leaks, the beams under the floor have rotted, and a
draft rattles the loose doors and windows. Capital repair is
needed, but we are satisfied with the fact that in one respect——
the showcase——everything has been done just as on a picture
postcard; everything is fine. We should be concerned about the

bricks and the lumber, but we spend our money only for paint and brushes, while we tirelessly chatter about our unique qualities as proprietors and about what terrible landlords our neighbors are.

Our country's proprietors have made a simple calculation: if only one percent of all the factories and plants in the country were clean on the outside and in technology, this would be more than enough for propaganda photographs, more than the most pedantic Western professor-pest could inspect.

The worse matters are with us in some area, then usually the more attention paid there to ideological issues, the fundamental advantages of socialism over capitalism, etc. This silly trait has now emerged in our approach to ecological problems. One need only to look on the shelves of the Lenin Library or the "public" libraries: the share of political and ideological questions among publications on nature conservation has increased sharply since 1974.[5]

Facts about "shortcomings" in matters of environmental protection in the USSR somehow get into books and articles, but they would never see the light if beforehand or afterward their authors did not make fundamental declarations about the basic superiority of socialism to capitalism in all respects, including ecology, and that the USSR has everything needed to quickly resolve all problems that come up. Experienced editorial personnel say that any feeble impulse to see the ecological crisis as a global, worldwide phenomenon, without continual mention of "two natures—capitalist and socialist," are unconditionally squelched. For example, a chapter in the book *Ecology: Policy and Law*, by O. S. Kolbasov, in which some of the shortcomings of Soviet laws on environmental protection were analyzed in connection with the overall socialist structure of society, never saw the light, even though, judging from the other chapters, the author is an absolutely loyal Marxist.

Many trustworthy authors who attempt to speak about the common course of the ecological crisis throughout the world and about the need to regulate the economies of different countries and regions in accordance with the counsels of the Club of Rome and other serious institutions are accused of anti-Soviet tendencies or "Sakharovism," which, for the censors, are the same thing. Yet to any normal person it is obvious that broad cooperation in ecological problems is now more important than the development of trade or even cultural relations. "If you don't think about your future, you will not have one," Galsworthy once observed. More than ever before, ecology now shapes the future of countries and peoples. Thus after disarmament, cooperation in the solution of ecological problems has become the most important aspect of international détente.

The more thoroughly ecological policy is kneaded with the yeasts of ideology, the less room remains for flexible economic decisions, for the exchange of valuable experience accumulated throughout the world.

The criticism of bourgeois theories and bourgeois practice in dealing with ecological problems is extremely superficial and opinionated and essentially cannot help solve similar problems in the USSR. What is most interesting in such books are the authors' slips. For example, V. Bartov calls the attempts of the renowned economist Wassily Leontief to introduce planning into the operations of American monopolies evidence of the total decay of bourgeois economic thought.[6] Bartov, a person who knows at first hand the results of the planning system in the USSR, probably assumes that only a madman or a suicide would attempt to do something similar in the United States.

The ideological approach to genetics and cybernetics did tremendous harm to Soviet science, and ultimately to the country's economic development. Abuses of ideology in the realm of ecological problems bear a different character, although they threaten even greater disasters. The solution or aggravation of ecological problems touches the very foundations of existence of all of society and not merely isolated, although important, areas of its operation.

In the words of Barry Commoner, who is quoted by Soviet ecologists more often than any other author, "condemning as anathema any suggestion which reexamines basic economic values; . . . burying the issues revealed by logic in a morass of self-serving propaganda . . . failing fully to inform citizens of what they need to know . . ."—all this is an intolerable luxury for human society if it wants to overcome the ecological crisis and survive.[7]

Deliberately distorted, embellished information pervades our society on all levels. The effects of those few steps that have been taken to preserve the environment have been diminished by the fact that they are conceived and implemented on the basis of false theories and statistics. Not only does the ordinary citizen see a distorted picture of ecological problems, but data sent "to the very top" are also colored to a different extent and for completely different reasons.

"We don't need an institute to show that the socialist system runs badly. We know it ourselves." So, evidently, stated a top leader about the Institute of Concrete Sociological Research of the Academy of Sciences, which was trying to do an objective study of sociological problems. Ecological investigations, like the forecasts *Nature 1980* and *Nature 1990*, which provide accurate data on the course of events, "round off" the results in their conclusions, pass them through a prism of ideological terms, and dilute them with the rose water of optimism, since everyone knows that "upstairs," in the government, they don't want to hear too much bad news.

Those governing the country can well imagine that if they fully unleashed citizens' personal initiative, if they slackened the reins of centralized planning, it would be possible to solve many problems of agriculture and industry. Many acute problems of ecology would be solved in the same way. However, people are not given full rein either creatively or legally. Their current position of servility, on all fours, suits our "best." Given such rules of the game, they always win however poorly they play. The price paid for our country's military and political power, for the esteem shown every representative of the Soviet government, for the respect with which every word uttered in the Kremlin is heard throughout the world, has been high. It includes the purity of unique Baikal and of dozens of rivers in the southern Ukraine and the Urals, the Sea of Azov, as well as the clarity of air in the Kuznets Basin and East Kazakhstan and the impoverishment of the soil in the Trans-Volga region and Kirghiz meadow lands. And ultimately it includes the health of the Soviet people, the health of generations to come.

Bertolt Brecht wrote about times when a conversation among three people about trees represented a lie, hypocrisy, since behind it stood silence about atrocities, about people innocently murdered. We live in an era when in journalists' innocent conversations about saving the eagle, the bison, or the beaver in our country one hears the silence about the destruction of thousands of other animals. It is a time when reliable facts about the multiplication of the saiga or muskrat prove false, since behind them are silence about the thousands of deer slaughtered by bullets and rockets, the soft cackle of the last of the vanishing red-breasted geese, and the screams of cranes and bustards. The propagandistic clamor about million-ruble treatment systems, about new fish-breeding farms, is meant to drown the silence of wasted forests, moribund Azov, and degraded Baikal.

Even the most innocent conversation about trees is no longer just a lie; it is almost a crime if it drops from the blossoming branches to the bole of the trunk, the point at which in our country they cut millions of trees whose destruction is a violation of all nature laws.

One of the staunchest defenders of nature, V. Chivilikhin, said not long ago that he would write nothing about nature conservation. "Such grave words now weigh on my mind," he said. "No one will permit them anyway. Who needs them?"

The government does not want to hear bad news "about nature," but people need this news. It is not political motives, not the dictates of reason—it is the very air we breathe that forces us to understand: if we want to survive, we must know the truth. And tell it to others.

# Notes

## Chapter 1: A Distant Cloud

[1] *October* [Oktiabr'], 1965, no. 4. A discussion of readers' letters on Chivilikin's essay about Baikal. His essay, entitled "The Radiant Orb of Siberia," was not only the first but also the most accurate statement about the Baikal tragedy.

[2] N. M. Zhavoronkov, academician, director of the Institute of Organic Chemistry of the Academy of Sciences, was concerned mainly with problems of the chemicals industry. Neither before nor since Baikal had he ever been concerned with anything even remotely resembling the problems of decomposition of organic matter, to say nothing of biochemical processes in rivers and lakes.

[3] *The Preservation of Siberian Mountainscapes* [Okhrana gornykh landshaftov Sibiri], Novosibirsk, 1973.

[4] Ibid.

[5] R. Shtilmark, *Taiga Fastnesses* [Taezhnye dali], Moscow, 1977.

[6] *Izvestia*, March 4, 1976.

[7] K. Mitriushkin, articles in the magazine *Hunting and Hunting Management* [Okhota i okhotnich'e khoziaistvo], 1977, nos. 3 and 11; the book *Man and Nature* [Chelovek i priroda], Moscow, 1974, etc.

[8] See K. Mitriushkin in the magazine *Hunting and Hunting Management*, 1977, no. 3.

[9] Guy Biolat, *Marxism and the Environment* [Marksizm i okruzhaiushchaia sreda], Moscow, 1976, translation from the French edition, *Marxisme et environnement*, Paris, 1973. To support the assertion that only Marxism will provide the correct solution to the environmental problem, Biolat refers to the experience of the USSR, "where a national park of 30,000 square kilometers (!) has been created around Baikal, and the construction of new factories around the lake has been prohibited (!)."

[10] Hundreds of books have been published about other aspects of the matter, especially the optimistic ones.

## Chapter 2: Secret Air

[1] MPC—maximum permissible concentration—is a standard for the content of toxic substances in the air, water, etc. In the air it is expressed in milligrams per cubic meter. For example, the Soviet standard for the concentration of carbon monoxide (CO) is 1 mg/cu m for a daily average and 3 mg/cu m for a spot test.

[2] For comparison: in highly industrialized Japan, which endured Hiroshima, the rate of genetic defects has reached 12 percent. Pollution—saturation with dust—of the atmosphere is a reason for the growing incidence of allergies. Today 2 percent of the country's population suffers from various kinds of allergies, and by 1990 this number will increase to 3.5 percent.

[3] In his review of the forecast *Nature 1980* [Priroda—1980], Academician Gerasimov wrote that the conclusions drawn by the authors of this report seem unconvincingly optimistic after the gloomy data they present throughout the text. Why, asked Gerasimov, do the authors claim that the measures taken in the Tenth Five-Year Plan will have a favorable effect on the state of nature in the Eleventh Five-Year Plan if they themselves show that the effect of these measures has been less than planned. He also criticized the forecast because it asks so little for nature conservation in the future. It is interesting that *Nature 1990* [Priroda—1990], in which Gerasimov himself was one of the leading figures, is similarly flawed. After describing the alarming situation in each area separately, in its conclusions the forecast uses such slick formulations that one might take them for an invitation to a wedding. And now Gerasimov's colleagues complain about the forecasts in *Nature 1990*: "The loss figures are underestimated. The results are glossed over."

[4] See *A Republic Conference: Current Problems in Environmental Protection* [Respublikanskaia konferentsiia: aktual'nye problemy okhrany okruzhaiushchei sredy], Tashkent, 1977. Health experts consider the pesticide Bazudin especially hazardous; it has a depressant effect on children and adults one kilometer from the edge of a cotton field that has been treated with it.

[5] W. Douglas, *The Three Hundred Year War* [Russian edition: *Trekhsotletniaia voina*, Moscow, 1975].

[6] According to statistics published in the USSR, investments in environmental protection by industry in the United States and Japan amount to 8 to 29 percent of all capital investments. In a few cases even we have allocated up to 30 percent of capital investments to the construction of "clean" oil refineries (for example, in Perm). But this was in special circumstances —for the showcase.

## Chapter 3: Secret Water

[1] B. Commoner, *The Closing Circle* [Russian edition: *Zamykaiushchiisia krug*, Leningrad, 1974]; retranslated from the Russian.

[2] Ibid; retranslated from the Russian.

[3] *Communist* [Kommunist], 1975, no. 17. The article by Professor M. Ia. Lemeshev.

[4] Ibid.

## Chapter 4: Secret Land

[1] *The Conservation and Improvement of the Environment* [Okhrana i uluchshenie okruzhaiushchei sredy], Tashkent, 1975. Figures of 15 to 20 percent are cited in other popular editions. American journalists, we have heard, were told 20 percent.

[2] K. P. Mitriushkin and L. K. Shaposhnikov, *Man and Nature* [Chelovek i priroda], Moscow, 1974.

[3] *Chemicals Industry* [Khimicheskaia promyshlennost'], 1977, no. 3.

[4] *NIITEKhim Information Survey* [Obzor-informatsiia NIITEKhim], 1976, no. 6.

[5] *Soviet Russia* [Sovetskaia Rossiia], September 24, 1977.

[6] See the article by Eligii Stavskii in *Literary Gazette* [Literaturnaia gazeta], September 17, 1975, etc.

[7] V. Zazubrin, speech at the First Congress of Siberian Writers, 1926.

[8] *Izvestia*, May 1, 1937. In his article Vs. Ivanov quotes Gorky's words about the new canals: "They are big rivers, my lord, and sane. Before rivers were mad."

## Chapter 5: The Law: Theory and Reality

[1] Having satisfactorily survived his first arrest in 1920, Vever continued to work at Gorky for four more years. Thereafter he occupied more important posts, until at a new stage in Russian history the "law" again caught up with him in 1937. It is not known whether the felled spruce figured in the charges, but it is known that in 1937 Vever was shot.

[2] *Literary Gazette*, March 23, 1977.

[3] The fact that the Ukraine is an equal member of the UN, as is the USSR, and Estonia is merely a sovereign republic of course makes no difference. In disregard for the rights of the republics, we must be given our due; we are very democratic: in the lack of rights all of us are equal.

[4] B. L. Muntian, in *The Twenty-second Congress of the CPSU and Problems of Collective Farm and Agricultural Law* [22-i s"ezd KPSS i problemy kolkhoznogo i zemel'nogo prava], Moscow, 1962.

[5] G. A. Aksenok, *Legal Problems of Environmental Protection in the USSR* [Pravovye problemy okhrany prirodnoi sredy v SSSR], abstracts of reports, Moscow, 1969.

[6] O. S. Kolbasov, *Ecology, Politics, Law* [Ekologiia, politika, pravo], Moscow, 1976.

[7] Dezhkin and Fetisov, *Profile of Equilibrium* [Profil' ravnovesiia], Moscow, 1977.

[8] N. Sladkov, *Miombo*, Moscow, 1977.

*Chapter 6: . . . Swans Like the Winter Snows*

[1] V. I. Iokhelson, *Essay on the Wild Animal Industry and Trade in the Kolyma Area* [Ocherk zverepromyshlennosti i torgovli v kolymskom okruge], Saint Petersburg, 1898.

[2] "Operation Cauldron" [Operatsiia kotel], *Literary Gazette*, August 4, 1976.

[3] *Hunting and Hunting Management*, 1977, no. 3.

[4] *Pravda*, July 5, 1977. Author—V. Prokhorov.

[5] In the steppes of Kazakhstan saiga are often exposed to radiation contamination from atomic tests. The contamination occurs not directly but through the grass and soil. Whole batches of dead saiga have been condemned in Tselinograd, Turgai, and other cities because of the high radioactivity in the meat.

[6] *Pravda*, September 27, 1976.

[7] We could continue such a chronicle of all the misfortunes befalling nature on the preserves for hundreds of pages. From the chronicler's viewpoint it is even better that we do not have so many preserves, that the percentage of preserve land in the USSR is only half that set aside in the United States and less than in any European country. And note that an abrupt increase of 100 percent in the area of preserves, as the United States is going to do, is impossible for us.

*Chapter 7: New Technologies*

[1] Report given by Vakula at the Conference on Waste-Free Technologies, Chernogolovka, 1977. The report also mentioned major achievements, the fact that whole branches of the chemical industry have shifted to "clean" technologies; but this is not the picture for the chemical industry as a whole.

*Chapter 8: New Ideas*

[1] Tupytsia and Petrov, *Information Issue of VNIITEIlesprom* [Informatsionnyi vypusk VNIITEIlesprom], Moscow, 1976.

[2] *Literary Gazette*, January 12, 1977.

[3] Yet the Ternei Logging Enterprise is one of the most "advanced" enterprises in the country! (*Lumbering* [Lesnaia promyshlennost'], 1977, no. 11.)

[4] *Pravda*, December 29, 1976.

[5] W. Douglas, *The Three Hundred Year War*, Moscow, 1975; retranslated from the Russian.

[6] Ibid.

[7] *Literary Gazette*, February 21, 1968.

[8] *Novy mir*, 1969, no. 10. "Science—the Source of Knowledge and Superstition" [Nauka—istochnik znanii i sueverii].

## Chapter 9: A Country in Reserve

[1] Here and in the following we use the term "Siberia and the North" to mean, as we have noted, Siberia without all the southern districts and the southern part of the Far East and all the European and Siberian North. More precisely, it is all the land to the north of the permafrost line.

[2] V. V. Kriuchkov, *The Delicate Subarctic* [Chutkaia Subarktika], Moscow, 1976.

[3] *Natural Resources of Yakutia* [Prirodnye resursy Iakutiia], Yakutsk, 1976.

[4] *The Preservation of Siberian Mountainscopes*, Novosibirsk, 1973.

[5] These figures—Odum's coefficient and the biological output of the countryside in Siberia and the North—make the calls for mass settlement of the Northeast unwarranted. Judging from the experience of modern Taimyr, with its one large city, Norilsk, one can say that one new Leningrad would turn the entire Northeast into a wasteland within the lifetime of a single generation. And then only provided that, like Norilsk, it would receive 80 to 90 percent of its products and goods from outside.

[6] *Komsomol Pravda*, August 10, 1971. "Sun and Midnight" [Solntse i polnoch'].

[7] Iu. M. Simchenko, *A Winter Route across Gydan* [Zimnii marshrut po Gydanu], Moscow, 1976.

[8] This is why foreign scientists and foreigners in general are finding it so hard to make contact with these peoples and to travel into the Soviet North. The naïve French ethnographer Malaurie several times tried to get to Chukotka; he probably believed the promises, but the people who had given them later told him frankly that aside from the Chukchis studying at the Leningrad Herzen Institute, Malaurie would see no Chukchis.

[9] *Some Problems of the Ethnogenesis and Ethnic History of the Peoples of the World* [Nekotorye problemy etnogeneza i etnicheskoi istorii narodov mira], Moscow, 1976.

[10] Shtilmark, *Taiga Fastnesses*, Moscow, 1977.

## Chapter 10: Taking Stock (Or: Who Will Pay for the Tragedy?)

[1] These figures include land whose biological productivity has been reduced by 80 to 90 percent and that can be restored to their former level only after 100 to 200 years. About 130 million hectares of plowland, 28 million hectares of meadow, and 160 million hectares of pasture land have undergone erosion. This totals 318 million hectares (3.18 million square kilometers), or almost half of the entire agricultural area of the country.

[2] *Communist*, 1975, no. 17.

[3] For comparison: in the United States the contribution to the growth of

national income is 30-35 percent. The contribution of education is roughly the same. For us education adds 6 percent.

[4] *Communist*, 1975, no. 17.

[5] In the period from 1975 to 1977 alone, books have been published on this subject by V. Bartov, V. Pavelev, N. Chichvarin, E. Girusov, O. Kolbasov, T. Grigorian, S. Gudozhnik, Guy Biolat, as well as collections by Leningrad State University, the Institute for World Economics and International Relations, Moscow State University, and so on. These publications constitute the broadest segment in the more general topic of ecology.

[6] V. F. Bartov, *Modern Capitalism and Nature* [Sovremennyi kapitalizm i priroda], Moscow, 1976, p. 216.

[7] B. Commoner, *The Closing Circle*, Leningrad 1974.

# Index

# About
# the Author

Boris Komarov is a pseudonym. The author is a ministry official who continues to live in the Soviet Union.

Marshall I. Goldman is Associate Director of the Russian Research Center at Harvard University and Professor of Economics at Wellesley College. He is the author of numerous books and articles on the Soviet economy and environment, including *The Spoils of Progress: Environmental Pollution in the Soviet Union*, *Ecology and Economics: Controlling Pollution in the '70s*, and *Detente and Dollars: Doing Business with the Soviets*.